T0114126

What People Are Saying

"I have seen people stand in line for hours just to get a moment with Deborah King. People just love her and her healing work."

— **Louise L. Hay,** the *New York Times* best-selling author of *You Can Heal Your Life*

"Deborah King is an amazing teacher with a powerful message. Spend a few minutes with her, and get ready for a paradigm shift!"

— **Marci Shimoff,** the *New York Times* best-selling author of *Happy for No Reason* and *Love for No Reason*

"Deborah King is an essential guide for all seekers of higher truth."

— **Neale Donald Walsch,** the *New York Times* best-selling author of *Conversations with God* and *The Only Thing That Matters*

"Deborah King is a spiritual guide to be reckoned with, and charismatic and entertaining to boot!"

— **James Van Praagh,** spiritual medium, TV host and producer, and *New York Times* best-selling author of *Ghosts Among Us*

"King's demonstration has been electrifying. . . . The next day I call her office to book a private appointment, which will prove to be the strangest, most exciting hour I've had in my yearlong experiment in alternative medicine, Hollywood style."

— **Kevin West,** editor of *W* magazine, from "Healing, Hollywood Style"

"Deborah King is a courageous and gifted healer."

— **Christiane Northrup, M.D.,** the *New York Times* best-selling author of *Women's Bodies, Women's Wisdom* and *The Secret Pleasures of Menopause*

ENTANGLED
in darkness

ALSO BY DEBORAH KING

*Be Your Own Shaman: Heal Yourself
and Others with 21st-Century Energy Medicine*

Truth Heals: What You Hide <u>Can</u> Hurt You

ENTANGLED
in darkness

SEEKING
the light

Deborah King

HAY HOUSE, INC.
Carlsbad, California • New York City
London • Sydney • New Delhi

Published in the United States by: Hay House, Inc.: www.hayhouse.
com® • *Published in Australia by:* Hay House Australia Pty. Ltd.:
www.hayhouse.com.au • *Published in the United Kingdom by:* Hay
House UK, Ltd.: www.hayhouse.co.uk • *Published in India by:* Hay
House Publishers India: www.hayhouse.co.in

Cover design: Amy Rose Grigoriou • *Interior design:* Pamela Homan
Interior photos: Eric Gignoux

Library of Congress Cataloging-in-Publication Data

King, Deborah
  Entangled in darkness : seeking the light / Deborah King. -- 1st ed.
      p. cm.
  ISBN 978-1-4019-3894-9 (hbk. : alk. paper) 1. Healing. 2. Energy
psychology. 3. Self-realization. 4. Mind and body. I. Title.
  RZ400.K548 2013
  615.8'51--dc23
                                            2012041089

Hardcover ISBN: 978-1-4019-3894-9
Tradepaper ISBN: 978-1-4019-7297-4
E-book ISBN: 978-1-4019-3896-3

1st edition, March 2013

Printed in the United States of America

❦ ❦

Aum Asato mā sad gamaya
Tamaso mā jyotir gamaya
Mṛtyormā amṛtam gamaya
(Bṛhadāraṇyaka-Upaniṣad I.iii.28)

From ignorance, lead me to truth;
From darkness, lead me to light;
From death, lead me to immortality.

❦ CONTENTS ❧

✧ INTRODUCTION ✧

*"Turn your face to the sun
and the shadows fall behind you."*

— MAORI PROVERB

It was the very last hour of the last day of a three-day workshop I was teaching in Arizona, and I was tired. I'd been out on a rigorous book tour for five months, and my fatigue was catching up to me. All of a sudden, as I was helping a student onstage with an issue, someone in the front row started to moan loudly. When I glanced down, I was surprised to see a case of what appeared to be partial possession in my student Lin Lin. I was so tired that I seriously considered ignoring it. Was it something I could handle in my current state of exhaustion? Because Lin Lin was a gifted aspirant and her heart was in the right place, I felt compelled to address it. Even though she was actively seeking the light and was in training to do healing work, somehow she had gotten connected to something dark.

As quickly as I could, I completed my work with the person on the stage and then stepped down to where Lin Lin was seated. At this point, she was literally roaring, throwing her head back and forth as in the movie *The*

Exorcist. Understandably, the audience members seated around her were uncomfortable. "This is not the real you," I gently explained to Lin Lin. "I know you're in there, though, and I really want to reach you. Would you like to be dissociated from this energy?"

"Yes, yes," she replied. "Please help me."

I began, and a real battle ensued. To bolster my strength, I called in every guide and pulled forth every resource I knew. It turns out that the "demon" that had infected my gifted student was an ancient dragon energy from her Chinese heritage. "You're okay," I reassured her. "You have in you a once-revered lineage that, although it was originally in the light, became dark after many years. You, however, are very attracted to the light. That's why you've come to this workshop. So, you can choose. This is entirely up to you. I want to encourage you to go to the light, but in order to do that, we will have to release this other energy."

With an "Okay," Lin Lin gave me her consent, and I worked to disconnect the dragon spirit from her. The possession in this case was very modest. Despite the fact that darkness was residing in her, it hadn't taken over completely.

The fact that this student worked in corporate America and was an educated and sophisticated modern gal didn't change the reality of carrying a darkness embedded within her psyche (although this was unbeknownst to her). After its removal, she said, "When I started to make those sounds—and they were just coming up and out of me of their own volition—I didn't know what they meant."

If you go back thousands of years in China when the energy was most active, this particular one was very much of the light. In fact, it was one of the highest on the planet at that time. And although that country's spiritual heritage was extremely high, it was susceptible to declining, becoming contaminated, and growing dark. Today, this same dragon energy is a low vibration, and by attaching itself to this student it was beginning to create a split in her that, if not removed, might ultimately block her life progress and spiritual development. With the studying and personal work Lin Lin had been doing, and her being present at a workshop in a roomful of light, this darker energy was coming forth to be seen and acknowledged so that it might be transmuted and released.

I wish this were an isolated incident, but as a healer who helps thousands of people, I do periodically encounter those in need of a partial or even full exorcism. These are frequently as dramatic as in Lin Lin's case and often scary, especially for those witnessing the depossession.

What sort of deal with the devil has a possessed individual or his or her ancestors made to attract such darkness? And what do these extreme dark events have to do with *you*, a seeker of the light?

Well, we are *all* on a pilgrimage of the soul. Life is a journey into higher consciousness, whether we're aware of it or not. This is how I see it: we come to this physical plane to be bearers of the light. By "the light" I mean the highest energetic frequency that exists in our world and from which we originate. This energy is sometimes called Source, Spirit, oneness, love, or God. You might think of this supreme vibration as the lofty peak of a mountain, where the air is fresh and you have a breath-taking, 360-degree view of creation. In fact, we often use mountain-related words like *pinnacle, peak,* and *summit* to describe the ultimate or most perfect state of something—in this case, the perfection of our essence, our consciousness.

When your soul incarnates and takes bodily form, your highest qualities—those associated with the light—come to reside in the *chakras* (energy centers) just above your head, where they are available to you. Every time you have a choice to take the high or low road, you can decide whether to manifest a higher or lower quality of character through your personality. For example, let's say a friend betrays you. What will you do in response? You can take the high road and choose the quality of forgiveness, or take the low road and react with spite and bitterness and plot to get even. Every day life offers you these opportunities to download those higher-vibration qualities you came here to make real. Those that you value and admire, which all stem from love, are stored in your higher chakras, and it's your task to start acting from them in your day-to-day activities.

Just as there is a higher self where these attributes are stored, there is inevitably also a lower self, where our more base ones reside—where there is light, there must be darkness. We come from the light, already *are* the light, and will someday merge back into oneness with the light, but we often forget this truth as we navigate through life. The part of us that does not remember our nature as a light bearer is our personal darkness. It shows up as our "issues"—our life challenges, childhood wounds, negative personality traits, and limited mind-sets. These aspects of ourselves disappoint or shame us, so we drive them into our unconscious where we don't have to acknowledge them, thus creating a dark side. In the case of those who are possessed, their dark side has been taken over by an outside force, because their personal darkness set them up to be vulnerable to it.

Although your dark side may be hidden from view, it always plays itself out in your life. It is fixated on physical safety and survival, and its traits, which stem from fear, constitute your propensity toward one or more of the seven deadly sins: lust, gluttony, greed, sloth, anger, envy, and pride. You might think of your lower self as the valley between two majestic mountain ranges. Indeed, one definition of the word *valley* is a place that is filled with fear, despair, or apprehension—a pretty good characterization of the lower self. We can watch the news and see one example after another of the dark side in action: the sports coach who turns out to be a pedophile, the movie star on drugs and alcohol who crashes her car, or the politician caught in a tawdry affair. We are all, it seems, made up of both light and dark.

Transforming Darkness

Until we become aware of the lesser qualities within ourselves and make a conscious choice to change them, they will continue to run our behavior, causing us disease and distress. Once we recognize that we have darkness, we can begin to bring it into our consciousness and transform it, which is the true meaning of healing.

Throughout my childhood, I lived with darkness. I was abused both emotionally and sexually by members of my family. And although as a child I'd connected deeply with the spiritual world through my family's Catholic faith, I abandoned that connection during my rebellious teenage years, replacing it with addictions—to alcohol, Valium, high-risk sports, and extreme dieting. I was also promiscuous and driven: as a young lawyer, I won cases by doing whatever it took, including attacking the other side fiercely and giving sexual favors to opposing counsel or the occasional judge. At age 24, I learned I was bipolar, and not long after got the news that I had cancer.

My diagnosis scared me. I didn't want to die. In fact, what I desperately wanted was a better way to live. I began reflecting as deeply as I could on my life and what might have caused me to become so ill. I promptly went to AA, which cleared my head. Next, I learned to meditate, which calmed me down and (along with AA) allowed me to stop much of the addictive behavior that was numbing the pain of my difficult childhood. I started to focus on caring for myself so that I could get well. As a result, my self-esteem began to improve, and I started to feel better. I tried alternative healing modalities like acupuncture and massage. Then, after several sessions with an energy healer, I had a "spontaneous" remission from the cancer. Realizing that this miracle was due in great part to the energy work I'd received, I became intrigued about how it worked, and my curiosity prompted me to take my first steps on the path to becoming a healer myself.

At that point, one of my addictions still lingered— cigarettes—and I no longer wanted to smoke. It simply didn't fit me anymore. I was concerned about the impact on my health, and, frankly, I found the habit to be socially awkward with the group of spiritual friends that I'd met through my newfound interests in meditation and healing.

It was the desire to quit smoking that sparked the idea of going to Nepal. I knew that when we break out of our routines and have the opportunity to see and learn something new, our mind-set can shift, and that this mental shift can be the very change that is needed to break an addiction or other negative habit. I surmised that a mountain-climbing trip to Nepal just might be the perfect cure for my smoking. After all, who can smoke in such rarified air?

I also had a second agenda for going to Nepal: I wanted to discover the secrets of spirituality and healing from the Tibetan Buddhist monks who lived high in the mountains there. In essence, I desired to climb to a higher level of consciousness. As is typical of me, once I get a notion about something, I feel there is no time to waste. So a few weeks later my husband, Eric, and I were on the tarmac in Kathmandu.

Reaching for the Summit

Climbing a mountain, like raising our consciousness, is work that many of us are spiritually driven to do. We *want* to reach that awesome summit; we *want* to reach that glorious light!

Eric and I were serious mountain climbers before we went to Nepal. (Located in the Himalayas, Nepal is home to eight of the world's ten tallest mountains, including Mount Everest—the highest point on the planet.) It was a journey that served as the perfect metaphor for the purpose of our existence here on Earth—to raise our consciousness and effect deep, soul-level healing, to disentangle from our darkness and live more in the light.

Exiting the airport, it felt like we had just landed in another world. While I'd been to exotic locales previously, and had done a considerable amount of third-world travel, Kathmandu seemed a lot more foreign than any place I'd ever visited. My husband and I took in the brilliantly colored prayer flags, the blaring horns, and the tantalizing smell of food cooking right there on the side of the road. The streets were filled in a chaotic fashion with people on foot and on bicycles, with yaks milling about. It took hours for our rickshaw to get from the airport to where we were staying our first night.

We planned to do the "vacation" portion of our trip first—scaling the 20,305-foot Island Peak that's adjacent to Everest—before devoting ourselves to our real pursuit of studying spirituality and healing. Having decided to tackle a mountain as high as Island Peak, we should have signed up with a reliable trekking group. However, full of pride in our climbing skills, we wanted to do it by ourselves. So we went out and, in pidgin English, hired a *Sherpa*, a young man who guides you up the mountain and back, buys the provisions—the rice and dried milk you're going to survive on—and arranges for more Sherpas to carry the cooking and sleeping gear.

The plane ride into Lukla from Kathmandu was the first step of our journey. I saw the pilot standing next to a little Canadian Twin Otter cargo plane as he smoked a cigarette and talked to his copilot while gassing up. That should have been a warning sign, but with a youthful sense of immortality coloring our view, Eric and I weren't the least bit deterred.

When the doors of the plane opened, ten of us—a mixed bag of international travelers—crawled in and sat cross-legged on the floor. I took the spot directly behind the pilot, with an expansive view out the front windshield. I was pleased with my position. With half a pilot's license under my belt and lots of time in the air in family planes, I thought I would be an experienced third set of eyes. But the pilot's credibility plummeted before we even got off the ground. Once the propellers were whirling, he pulled out a large bottle of rum and took a drink, and then leaned back and told us, "Pass it around!"

The weather that day was miserable; I couldn't see a thing. To make matters worse, I noticed that the plane had no instrument-landing capability. After about an hour in the air, I got to see just how skilled the pilot was. Without a hint of warning, he suddenly forced the plane's nose downward, as one might witness at an air show. From what I could see out the windshield, we were headed straight for the ground! I was gripped by horrendous fear as the earth rose up to meet us. Then, just as suddenly as before, the pilot pulled the plane's nose back up mere seconds before we would have crashed. I was astonished to see a little dirt runway stretching out in front of us that led uphill. Thankfully, we landed directly on it, and the small plane rolled to a stop. I had never been so relieved. I began to realize just how lucky we were when I looked around and saw crumpled remnants of other Twin Otters strewn across the hillside. I turned to Eric and said, "We're *not* flying out of here!" (Later I learned that this particular airport is rated the most dangerous in the world.)

Thus began the highs and lows of our adventure in Nepal. In Lukla, we joined our Sherpa, and the three young women, called Sherpinas, who would carry our belongings mounted on the tops of their heads. The entire journey—to the summit and back—was arduous and exhausting. The land was never flat, nor was it just straight up; it was always up and down, up and down. The bad part about that, of course, is when you turn around to come back, you have to go up and down, up and down all over again.

Our regimen was to trek all day for seven or eight hours, walking as far as we could before stopping for the night. If we ended up near a village—usually a tiny, three-hut settlement—we would ask the locals for food and a place to sleep. Even though these individuals had so little in the way of material goods, they were always generous—giving us their only two eggs, for example, or the few potatoes they had spent the whole day digging up in a field. Water was especially scarce, as the only source was thousands of feet below in a gorge. It had to be carried up the mountain by the women, using a tree limb across their shoulders, with a bucket suspended on either end. (I noticed that the women seemed to do almost all of the manual labor in Nepal.) Despite their hardships, the people of the region were welcoming, and their lives seemed to be filled with pure joy. I had never seen anything like it.

At night, when we slept in their huts, the air would be full of thick, black smoke from the cooking fire. The hut would also be filled with animals: yaks, goats, and any other treasured beasts were brought inside and cared for like family members, as they were heavily depended upon for their milk and wool. Then, just as we'd settle down, the family member who was the priest in the group would start his vigil, saying prayers and spinning a prayer wheel throughout the night. Needless to say, a restful night's sleep was hard to come by.

Since water was such a luxury, one particularly difficult aspect of the journey, at least at first, was that these people never bathed. We would sit around the fire with the wizened old matriarch who had never had a bath or even washed her hands in her life. In a culture such as this, where it's a punishable offense for a woman to be in public without her clothes, bathing in a stream is not an option. As one might assume, our delightful hosts had quite a pungent odor. But after being there only a few weeks, Eric and I stopped noticing and, thankfully, were equally as unaware of our own strong scent.

So there we were, eating food prepared by unclean hands and drinking water that could not be boiled long enough to be purified at such a high altitude, keeping our fingers crossed that we wouldn't become infected with hepatitis. We did get horrible dysentery, the inconvenience of which was compounded by a lack of plumbing or even toilet paper. It was like going back thousands of years. At the time of our trip, cell phones and the Internet didn't yet exist, and in such a remote region of Nepal there was no TV, radio, or even roads or cars. The villagers didn't have money or careers. These people were truly living off the land, and by traipsing off to this mostly unsettled part of the world my husband and I were truly putting ourselves in a precarious situation. If we were to get sick, we were weeks from even the most primitive form of medical care.

Amazingly, after about ten days in these crude conditions, I'd reached an entirely new state of being: I no longer worried about safety or sanitation, and I didn't know or care what time it was. Along with my cigarettes, I'd relinquished my watch back in Kathmandu. I lapsed into the mentality of the place and, for the first time in my life, was living 100 percent in the present moment. Much to my surprise, I found the Nepalese way of life to be much more satisfying than what I'd left behind in the U.S. These people cared only about the beauty of the sunrise and the stunning mountain views. The whole experience was incredibly freeing for me.

As we made our way up the mountain, we'd occasionally come to a holy shrine, which according to custom we were to walk around to the left. At about 12,500 feet, we stopped at the famous Tengboche Monastery and met the Buddhist monk who was its resident seer. He blessed us on our journey—the tradition for climbing teams attempting one of those peaks.

On the way up to the summit, the air gradually got much colder and thinner, and at about 18,000 feet I began experiencing altitude sickness. While I was already an accomplished climber—having done high-altitude work in the Alps—Nepal was much, much higher, and it didn't help that we'd violated the cardinal rule about climbing slowly. I developed a sleep disorder that's common at these heights due to the altitude and your slower pulse rate—the moment you fall asleep, your respiration slows to the point that you momentarily stop breathing and wake up suffocating and screaming, similar to sleep apnea. I would knock the tent down in my half-awake panic three or four times a night, which was exhausting. Finally, at 19,000 feet I had the sense to turn around and begin the long, up-and-down descent back to 12,000 feet, where I could once again breathe.

The climb back down was as full of adventure as the journey up had been. We got lost numerous times, and it took us weeks longer than anticipated to find our way out. As difficult as these experiences were in the moment, I learned to love them for what they taught me about resilience, resourcefulness, and simply surrendering to what is. In fact, the journey back down was the more spiritually focused part of our pilgrimage, and we found ourselves back at the Tengboche Monastery. We spent a great deal of time with the seer there, receiving his training. He and his fellow monks took great care to teach me how to pray, use a prayer wheel properly, and drop into the right space to truly connect with the Divine, which they did by chanting. I had a wonderful time with these wise men and learned things that changed my life and advanced me as a healer.

By the time Eric and I arrived back on foot in Kathmandu, we had each lost nearly 30 pounds but had received much enlightenment. We were also covered from head to toe with flea bites from our nights in the huts. More than anything, I couldn't wait to sit on a chair instead of on the ground, as the chair, too, was rare above Kathmandu.

As difficult as the trip had been, I'd accomplished what I'd set out to do—to quit smoking and learn profound lessons that raised my consciousness from the Buddhists: about simplicity, how less is more, and how to stop thinking about time altogether. Before this experience, I'd been obsessed with time—I was a true type A Westerner for whom "more," "faster," and "sooner" were always better. In Nepal, I learned how to tap into the hidden life of Spirit and to spend time there, elevating my vibration and my consciousness in the process.

As I mentioned, the path up Island Peak was neither flat nor straight; we had to climb up *and* down to get to the summit. Likewise, the journey to higher consciousness is one of ups and downs—toward the light and away from it. In other words, at times we act from our higher self and at other times from our lower self, but we hope our overall trajectory is up, toward the light. As we go up, it's important to have the proper foundation and to recalibrate our energy field to handle the increasing vibration. Again, this is just like mountain climbing, where breathing can be very difficult unless you gradually acclimate to greater heights.

As I learned while climbing in Nepal, when we draw on our inner resources to reach the mountain's peak, we discover what we're really made of. Likewise, it's through meeting the challenges of our darkness—our issues, problems, and pain—that we recognize our true nature as light. That's what we're going to do here: look at the darkness from a place of love, the way I loved even the difficulties we encountered on the mountain, so we can move more into the light.

In This Book

Now I would like to show you how to recognize and untangle your personal darkness and increase your ability to live in the light, thereby raising your consciousness. You will learn how to connect with the Divine, and you don't even have to climb a mountain in Nepal to do it. You can stay right at home and learn from a book like this one, attend a workshop, or study with a spiritual teacher, as being in the presence of someone who is more highly evolved pulls you up to a higher level of consciousness. (After all, the resident seer at Tengboche Monastery not only elevated my vibration, the blessing he offered me on the way up quite possibly gave me the good sense to turn around when I did and helped me back down the mountain when I was suffering from altitude sickness.)

We're going to take a stroll on the dark side to look at the nature of our own shadow, investigate the dark energy that can get aimed in our direction, and discover the keys to avoid generating more darkness. We'll also take a look at what happens when someone is possessed by darkness, and then we'll climb up into the light. From there, we'll head into the world of healing with the light and find out what that really means. We'll look at what happens when those who were once in the light fall from grace into darkness and what can happen when we fail to do our inner work in this life as we prepare for the ultimate initiation—our own death. Finally, we'll look at mental darkness and address ways in which to avoid it and live in the light.

You'll receive the incentives and tools necessary to stay steady on the path toward higher consciousness so that you can enjoy a greater knowledge of yourself; a greater sense of well-being in both physical and emotional health; and the incredible joy and peace that come from ridding yourself of darkness, bringing in more light, and sharing that light through your unique gifts with the rest of the world.

As the prayer from the Upanishads says, "From darkness, lead me to light." May this book help guide you in that direction.

CHAPTER ONE

The Forces of Darkness

"Darkness cannot drive out darkness:
only light can do that.
Hate cannot drive out hate:
only love can do that."

— MARTIN LUTHER KING, JR.

We are all entangled in darkness—those frailties, issues, and wounds that we relegate to our unconscious because we find them unacceptable to our self-image. The problem with this method of dealing with our darkness is that denial not only doesn't make it go away, but it gives it more power, too. When you plant a seed in the earth, or when an embryo is held and nourished in the darkness of the womb, it grows. But rather than a flower blooming or an infant being born, when the shadow side of the psyche is kept hidden, what is the fruit of that seed? More virulent darkness.

Just as the plant pushes up through the soil to reach the beneficent rays of the sun, your shadow side seeks the light. How will it do that? By calling your attention to it. Your unresolved issues and tendencies to the dark side reach out to you by manifesting as the obstacles you encounter in life. Are you having trouble paying the rent? Do you have a difficult relationship? Are your kids giving you grief? Is your health an issue? These are the types of challenges that shake up your complacency and allow you to find the areas in your life that need to be healed. You transform your inner darkness by exposing it to the light. That's why the dark dragon energy in my student Lin Lin made such a dramatic appearance after three days of a light-infused workshop: it was seeking to be released.

It's never a matter of "if" we have darkness within; it's always a matter of "how much." How much darkness or light a person holds has a great deal to do with how hard he or she works to transform the darkness and bring in more light. As you will learn, even those who are very much in the light can peak and then fall into darkness, just as the ancient dragon energy had over the centuries. The amount of darkness we hold also has to do with how much we avoid the things that make us darker, like the negativity of others that gets directed our way, trade-offs that we know are wrong but we make for our own gain, and supernatural forces of evil that latch onto us when we leave the door open for them. Rather than being afraid of the dark—which is a completely natural reaction—seek to understand it better so that you may recognize it when it confronts you.

To begin, let's look at our vulnerability to an attack of darkness by another. I call this *psychic attack,* and it comes in different forms and in varying degrees of intensity.

Psychic Attack

You've probably noticed that your life issues, your core wounds, are where you feel most vulnerable. These are the places where your buttons get pushed and you're quickest to raise your defenses. If you're overweight, for example, are you embarrassed and ashamed when you overhear someone say that you're "heavyset"? If you find out your partner is having an affair, do you fall into jealousy and anger? If you lose your job, do you feel worthless? These reactions are emotional, but much is going on energetically, too. Your wounds, the areas where you are the least protected, exist as weaknesses, as holes in your energy field that leave you open to attack.

Most people are unconscious of the ways in which they spread their negativity. They lack the self-awareness to recognize their own jealousy (the most common form of darkness), their desire for power and control, or their greed. Instead of dealing with the underlying sense of inadequacy and low self-worth that make them envious of anyone with a better body; a more loving partner; or a bigger paycheck, house, or car, they vent their jealousy the only way they know how—by acting out. They take their negative feelings and project them outward, blaming *others* for their own problems. This is psychic attack.

Even though I talk about this topic elsewhere in my writings, no discussion of the dark side of life would be complete without some mention of it. Here are the general categories of psychic attack I most commonly see:

— *Energy vampire* is a term that refers to individuals who suck energy from others, fueling themselves by siphoning someone else's life force. While some people depict energy vampires as sinister, supernatural presences, I have found them to be very human, highly needy beings. They didn't receive enough love as children, so they are always feeling slighted; they seek attention and validation from others because they're unable to give it to themselves. When you encounter an energy vampire, you usually wind up feeling drained.

Energy vampires are annoying, to say the least, but the damage from an encounter with one is usually minimal. That being said, I recommend avoiding them as much as you can. If you do have to spend time with one, don't indulge his or her neediness. Don't let a coworker corner you so she can complain about her list of ailments in order to get your sympathy. If you can't avoid her, gently suggest that she see someone who can help with her problems. She will stop being an energy vampire when she faces her problems and takes positive action.

— *Slime* is the next level of psychic attack, and the most common. It can slip right through a hole in your energy field and throw you off balance. It might be something as seemingly insignificant as an unpleasant phone call or e-mail, or even a harsh look, but you'll feel the effects. You may lose your focus, get confused or slightly depressed, or become jumpy and irritated without knowing why. All energy vampires slime you, but not all slime is of the vampire type; sometimes slime pushes at you rather than pulls from you, as an energy vampire does. Maybe one of your friends calls and relays some negative gossip about someone you both know, and as a result you feel disgusted for even listening and confused about what to do with the information. You've been slimed.

Slime can be remedied fairly easily by taking a clearing bath; you can also clear a room or other space of negative energy by burning a solution with Epsom salts. For specific instructions on the clearing bath and how to clear a space, please visit **www.deborahkingcenter.com/clearing**.

— *Cords,* or streamers of auric light, connect us to each other through our chakras and are formed with the implicit consent of both parties. They're naturally present in relationships. There are good cords, as in the love that connects the heart chakras of a parent and child or of two friends. Then there are bad cords, which are used to control or harm others. These negative cords have different effects on the recipient, depending on the chakra being corded. For example, if the fifth chakra is corded to silence you, you might start to stutter or become painfully shy. Once a good one is established, it can go bad if negative emotions such as jealousy arise.

Cords are not always easy to disconnect, but you can release the less serious ones yourself using a powerful shamanic technique. (I offer this exercise in my book *Be Your Own Shaman.*) You can also have an experienced energy healer disconnect your cords, which is necessary for the more serious ones, such as those that are involved in any kind of physical, emotional, or sexual abuse.

— A *vector of force* is a stream of energy one level more severe than a cord. Unlike cords, a vector can enter a hole in your energy field without your consent. Victims of vectors will often complain of a loss of control in some area of their life and may feel "stuck." Vectors are always dark, and they are very difficult for a recipient to disconnect from without some help. For example, a woman at a recent workshop complained of horrific migraine headaches that had begun when she started dating a new boyfriend. As it turned out, she had a vector that came from a quasi-religious cult, of which her boyfriend was a member. In a cult, a vector is a means of controlling people. Fortunately, hers came out, and she soon broke up with her boyfriend. Vectors always require professional help for removal, as do possessions.

— *Possession,* unlike the psychic weapons that stem from people attacking others, comes from the supernatural realm. This is not some urban legend or mystical tall tale, nor is it simply the imagination of Hollywood filmmakers. Having witnessed and dealt with hundreds of cases of both partial and full possession, I can attest that they are real and that they exist now as much as at any other time in human history. Most individuals these days would look at someone who is possessed and assume that he or she has a mental illness; indeed, it is difficult to distinguish between the two, but they are, in fact, different. I spent many years training with experts in exorcism and now teach my students at special seminars how to tell the two conditions apart and what to do about each.

Although the vast majority of people will never come in contact with a case of possession, you should be aware that this dark force exists so you can protect yourself should you happen to encounter it. (We will explore possession more thoroughly in the next chapter.)

Fending Off the Dark Side

The best way to deal with psychic attack is to avoid it. For many years as a practitioner, I was very careful to sidestep dark energy. There is nothing wrong with saying, "I don't have enough training for this," and steering clear of it. If you're not sure how to handle a situation, turn away from it as fast as you can. If you're unable to avoid interacting with an individual who's filled with dark energy, there are a few precautions you can take to protect yourself or to clear yourself after an attack has occurred.

As with our physical health, prevention is the best medicine. It's always much harder to clear out a psychic attack *after* the damage has been done. The best way to keep your energy clear, light, and flowing strong is to process and release your own thoughts and emotions so they don't lodge in your energy field and increase your personal quotient of darkness. The blocks, sludge, and holes in your field permit the darkness of a psychic attack to get in. As with a strong immune system, the healthier your field is, the less likely you are to be affected when you come into contact with the negativity of others.

Of course, everyone is a work in progress. As long as you're alive, there will be issues to work through and resolve. Inevitably, you'll experience some weaker moments. Therefore, as a second means of defense, it can also be extremely helpful to have the ability to *sense* dark energy so you can be on the alert when it's headed your way. Also, if you're interested in any of the healing arts, sensing energy—both dark and light—is crucial. And if you're involved in any kind of spiritual pursuit, being able to recognize it can help you distinguish whether someone or something is of the light, as the following story illustrates.

Too Close for Comfort

After I had spoken to a group in France, the man who sponsored the talk approached me. He was handsome, wore a custom-made suit, and was obviously affluent. He thanked me for coming, said he was impressed with my presentation, and wanted to show me his collection of rare esoteric documents from Egypt. He hinted that he wanted to set up a charitable organization for my work and make a big donation. He offered to have a car and driver pick my husband and me up in the morning to take us to his estate. Even though he had seemed quite dark to me in that first brief meeting, I was intrigued and agreed to go. As is often the case, curiosity got the better of me.

The next morning, we were driven to his beautiful estate, perched on the top of a hill overlooking a valley. As our car pulled into the grand circular driveway, the man's lovely wife came out to greet us. Everything looked normal, yet I felt a considerable amount of trepidation. When the man opened the front door and escorted us in, every hair on my body stood straight up. *Oh my God,* I thought. *I don't know what's going on here, but this feels dangerous!*

The man led us deeper into the house. The farther we went, the darker it felt and the more my feelings of apprehension grew. I finally became so uncomfortable that I started looking for an exit. In a back room filled with books, documents, and artifacts, he showed us papers that he said went back to ancient Egypt and the pyramids. Although he was convinced that it was all very holy, I could tell that he had, in fact, stumbled upon something extraordinarily dark and it had latched onto him. I couldn't wait to get out of there. It was truly one of the darkest energies I have ever encountered. I said a quick, "It was really nice to have met you . . . ," then almost jumped through a window in my hurry to leave. I hardly even said good-bye.

Once I was safely back in the car, I realized that this man thought he was dealing with ancient artifacts from some very holy sect, when actually he had an extremely dark energy attached to the documents that was invading his consciousness. Pride in his material possessions had created the opening. As you can see, it can be critical to be able to recognize and deal with your own dark side if you don't want to be contaminated or sucked in by another's darkness. You don't want to make your own deal with the dark.

Making Deals with the Dark

All day, every day, we are making choices. Do I eat a granola bar or eggs for breakfast? Should I go out to lunch with Cindy or stay in? Can I find someone to pick up the kids so I can get to the gym, or do I skip it yet again? While on the surface these decisions may seem insignificant or merely about practical matters, they are actually spiritual choices that affect the level of your vibration and consciousness. Eggs are better for your body than a food that's more like a candy bar. Cindy has all the earmarks of an energy vampire. And if you don't get to the gym, how are you going to deal with your stress? On this plane of free will, everything counts. Each decision either raises you up energetically or lowers your vibration.

The goal, of course, is to bring in more light. You always want your energy field expanding, not contracting or becoming muddy or dim. Darkness in your field can eventually become sickness in the body and mind. When you make a choice that brings you down energetically, you are in essence making a deal with the dark side, which then only attracts more darkness to you. Here are some examples of choices that have the potential to become dark deals:

- ୭୧ *Am I going to tell the truth, or am I going to lie? A teeny, tiny white lie can't hurt.*

- ୭୧ *Am I going to go along with this so I can reap the rewards, even though I know it's wrong?*

- ୭୧ *Am I going to sell him out so I'll get promoted?*

- ୭୧ *Am I going to exclude her so that I can feel better about myself?*

- ୭୧ *Am I going to abuse my power here because I know I can?*

- ୭୧ *Am I going to stay in this marriage or job out of guilt or greed?*

We make trade-offs like these all the time. We manipulate others to get our own way. We'll do *this* in exchange for *that*. We decide that we won't speak up for our co-worker who is being blamed for something that isn't his fault; by keeping silent, we increase our chances of getting his job. Ask yourself, "What am I *really* trading for that 401(k)? Am I giving up a piece of my integrity for that little white lie to my partner? What compromises am I making to keep my family's approval? Am I burying my head in the sand on an important issue, refusing to take a stand I know I need to take?" Each decision is a deal with the dark or with the light. Nothing is neutral. Nothing goes unrecorded on your karmic slate in your soul's evolution.

So where are *we* making a deal with the dark? This can be difficult to see, especially if we're not used to paying attention to our thoughts and motives. Most of us are not aware of the myriad choices we make each and every day. Even if we're conscious in the moment that we make a deal with the dark, that increased darkness generally gets split off into our shadow or unconscious side. Often, we won't admit our darkest deals until much, much later—if and when we are ready to return to the light.

Dark deals can come in a million different forms and varieties, but here's one I'm sad to say I frequently see. My client Sharon was in love with a new man and felt that marrying him would ensure that she wouldn't have to be alone, a prospect that terrified her. In exchange, she put up with his horrendous emotional and physical abuse of her little girl from her first marriage. Years later, she paid dearly for this decision when he dumped her. When she tried to reunite with her now adult daughter, the girl would have nothing to do with her. Sadly, the daughter had turned to drugs and was living a life of hopelessness and addiction. My former client's deal was a dark one indeed, and the result was a tragedy for all involved. That's the way it works. The darker the deal, the darker our lives become.

We all make deals with the darkness now and then. It keeps us humble when we realize what has happened. Here's something that happened to me recently that really brought me to my knees in the face of evil.

The Price of Ignoring My Intuition

I had just finished a powerful workshop on the East Coast when I was asked to give a private session. (I hadn't done one in nearly ten years, but had just announced that I'd be regularly doing a few every month.) Under the circumstances, my staff was hard-pressed to say no to this very persistent caller. She was obviously affluent, wanting to fly in from a foreign country on her private jet just to see me.

In order to do the work I do, I have to be in self-awareness 24/7. At the time, I remember noticing a slight feeling of self-importance that this woman would come so far just to see me for an hour—not a good state of mind for a healer. We need to come from a place of total humility in order to remove darkness and bring in the light. So, there was the first warning sign that I might not be in the correct alignment—that is, directly connected to Spirit in order to effect a change in physical, emotional, or spiritual bodies—and able to protect myself from any dark forces. Any thoughts or emotions that could negatively affect one of my own chakras (in this case, pride, which can distort both the third and seventh chakras) can take me out of alignment, make my work less effective, and make me vulnerable to negative energy.

Then there was a second warning sign: I had woken up that day with a little cold and actually shouldn't have been working at all. There's no way you can heal others when you're even slightly sick; this work requires your energy field *and* your body to be in super shape. In order to serve others, I need to look out for me first. Despite this second solid reason to back out, I continued moving forward, not wanting to disappoint this woman (again, this is not a valid motivation—the need for approval is a distortion of the third and fourth chakras).

Then, to top it off, as a special accommodation because of the long distance this client was traveling, I agreed to see her later than I normally work in the evening. Here was warning sign number three that I should have heeded. I was ignoring my own safety rules.

So while all these thoughts were floating around in my awareness, the woman walked into the room . . . and every hair on my body stood up. It was almost dark outside, and the room was barely lit by a small lamp. The first thing I noticed were her eyes—without any doubt the most disturbing eyes I've ever seen! They were shining so brightly in the half-light that I gasped. I seriously considered jumping out the nearest window, which I have actually done on a few occasions when I knew the evil that was present was beyond my skill level. But my guest immediately offered the explanation that serious medical issues had necessitated complex eye surgery a few years previously. The details were pretty grim, as the surgery involved removing her eyeballs and digging bigger sockets in her skull.

If there's one thing I know about dark energy, it's to never look it straight in the eye. Those who had the chance to work with me at the Intensive on Mental Health and Illness in Los Angeles (if you'd like to see that workshop, it's available at **www.deborah kingcenter.com/healingthemind**) know that I always teach my students to stand behind it or at an angle to avert their gaze. But after my guest told me about her surgery, I kept looking straight into her eyes, stupidly trying to figure out if that incredible feeling of trepidation and danger I was getting was a signal to run for the hills or simply the result of the difficult procedure she'd endured.

I kidded myself that my perceptions were a bit off at that moment, because I wasn't entirely well and the hour was late. In fact, I was ignoring my initial strong intuitive hit that pure evil was staring me in the face. (Your first instinct is always your best; once your left brain starts thinking, you're going to get confused. Your left brain simply doesn't have the immediate kind of accurate knowing that your right, intuitive brain does.) So, for a variety of reasons—and even though I know way, way better—I talked myself into thinking that her eyes were terrifying simply because she'd had surgery. In addition, I didn't want to have to go through the embarrassment of telling her that I couldn't (or wouldn't) help her. Despite being fully aware of my thoughts, I still moved forward for all the wrong reasons. I was definitely out of alignment!

While I was having all these thoughts, this gal was telling me a complicated medical story that involved problems with her feet. She was wearing a long skirt that completely covered her legs and feet, so I couldn't see them. But when she got up on the massage table and I uncovered them, I was horrified to find that she had cloven hooves! Seriously! Each foot had a separation between the big toe and the rest of the foot, which was one solid piece. Now, we all know that cloven hooves are a sign of the devil, and I absolutely wanted to run out of the room at this point, realizing that I was indeed in the presence of full-on demonic possession, as I had originally suspected. I've done more than my fair share of depossessions, or exorcisms, and I know that I have to be healthy, rested, and in total alignment to be safe, yet I was none of those things. But by time I saw her feet, I was too far gone to take care of myself. Foolishly, I just kept working, thinking about how she had flown some 20 hours to see me. I'd made a deal with the dark energy: I'll stay with this woman long enough so I look good.

The moment she left the room, I started feeling very dizzy. I couldn't even stand up, and I knew I was in big trouble. My husband, Eric, who's always nearby, raced me out of there and took me to a local acupuncturist, who took one look at me and said, "You're really sick; you better go straight to a hospital." When the acupuncturist gives up on you, you're in trouble! At the hospital, I found out that I had some sudden and mysterious bacteria that was morphing into pneumonia. I, who hadn't taken an antibiotic in over 30 years, was suddenly on two of them!

So why did I get so sick? When we're out of alignment, we develop small holes in our personal energy field. The feelings of pride and not wanting to look bad, coupled with being physically weak due to the illness I was fighting off, created holes in my field. Some of this woman's dark energy oozed out of her and seeped into me, making me very sick. Evil is real, and it needs to be treated very carefully. I let my guard down and had to deal with the consequences.

I spent many years studying exorcisms with a variety of priests, ministers, and shamans; I saw many of them get sick, and some even suffered an early demise. I know what to do, as I'm highly trained in this field, and yet I did everything wrong and for the wrong reasons. And I certainly paid for it.

Afterward, for additional clearing, I consulted a fellow teacher who works in the Zen Buddhist tradition. He reminded me that I have a very old pattern from many lifetimes of blaming myself and carrying a lot of shame. My guest had triggered this issue, and I went into an archetype of being powerless and was captured by the glittering darkness. The woman was carrying heavy, negative karma, and when I was confronted by her darkness and looked straight into it, I became mesmerized and disempowered. I felt impotent—unable to flee.

The good news? The experience caused me to heal at an even deeper level, and I survived and was able to come back and tell you all about it. Do be very careful when handling darkness. Be sure you err on the side of caution, get plenty of training, and are totally in the light if you choose to confront it!

The Ability to Sense Dark Energy

Even when I was young, my ability to recognize the darkness was always strong. A childhood fraught with emotional and sexual abuse makes a person hyper-sensitive to the dark side of life. But as I always point out, the experience of abuse turned out to be a real strength for me as a spiritual teacher and healer, because it has enabled me to tune in to the endless variation in degrees of light and dark that I encounter every day. It's a real benefit for aspiring healers to be exposed both to the light and the dark; as healers, they will need experience working with both.

I have a staunch practice of going into every situation I can with a clean slate—without being influenced by the opinions or experiences of others—so that I can get my own untainted read. I do this even with people I've previously met and places I've visited before, since it's always possible for a person or place that was once in the darkness to head to the light, or vice versa. Never assume that anything is permanently full of light or totally lost in darkness. When you encounter anything—new or old—try the clean-slate approach: a mind-set of curios-ity and wonder that allows you to be fully in the pres-ent. With this approach, life simply unfolds while you observe it as it really is, without any preconceptions or filters from your past distorting what you see. This really enhances your innate sensing abilities.

However, when you're first learning to develop these skills, it's helpful to receive guidance from someone sea-soned in recognizing energy. I encourage my students to learn the same way I did—from teachers asking me to notice how my body responded when something was happening in the workshop. I talk about what I'm sensing as a situation is occurring so that my students can compare their impressions with mine. During my weekly radio show and in workshops, I often comment on whether something is of a high or low vibration, light or dark, or grounded or ungrounded before I ask, "What are *you* sensing?"

When darkness presents itself at one of my presentations, a palpable energy can be felt in the room. Recently, as I was just finishing a talk, I asked if anyone else in the audience wanted to be helped. I saw a young woman walking from the back of the room, and as she drew closer, I noticed the temperature in the air dropping. At the same time, the lights began to flicker. My own body also gave me sensations that I recognize as the presence of evil approaching. Often I will ask participants to notice how their bodies respond to the presence of a dark energy such as this. That way, whenever they feel the same thing in their own lives, they will know it means that a dark energy is present and they need to be extremely cautious.

Our bodies never lie, and each person has his or her own unique warning system. You'll want to know yours intimately, as it can always be trusted to guide you to what's real and true. We all have different responses to the same stimuli. For example, I learned that for me a light, bubbly, champagne-like feeling in my body indicates the presence of a positive, high vibration, while an energy that raises goose bumps combined with a feeling of dread means a darker energy is afoot. Interestingly, both very high and very low energies give me goose bumps, although it's easy for me to distinguish between the two. If I'm sensing a high energy, my body responds by wanting to float or fly; with the bad goose bumps, I automatically start to bend my knees deeply and summon a strong connection to Mother Earth as well as call in shamanic guides to support me. I also get a strong urge to remove the dark energy from the space or from the person where I'm sensing it, in order to let in more light.

Your own bodily responses will be unique to you. The important thing is to note what your body is doing, so that you can discern dark from light when it presents itself to you. To do that, you have to trust your intuition.

Honoring Your Intuition

The ability to detect darkness or light in people and places is an extension of your ordinary senses. The tool is your intuition, and you're probably already somewhat adept at using it. Maybe you know, for example, when a place has bad vibes. For example, you arrive at a party and decide to leave after only a few minutes. You might not know why, but you turn to your partner and say, "I don't like the way this feels." Perhaps you walk into a house or apartment and know that you'd never want to live there.

As you start to listen to your intuition, you'll refine it and make it stronger—that is, as long as you honor it. It's crucial that you not ignore the prompts your intuition gives you, or it will weaken and go dormant. It's interesting that as children we are often very intuitive, but as we get older we tend to shut that ability down. We may feel that it hasn't actually helped us stay out of harm's way, because we don't yet have the power to control some of the negativity in our lives.

To keep your intuition working optimally and giving you the information you need, not only to stay safe but also to get insights about the next steps that might be valuable for your healing and evolution, honor this invaluable gift. It's actually your strongest sense, even more important than your intellect, which can easily lead you astray. Your intuition is your greatest ally in helping you avoid the darkness in others and fine-tune your awareness of your own darkness. By honoring your intuition and staying attuned to yourself, you'll be far less likely to fall into the trap of trying to suppress your emotions through destructive coping mechanisms such as addiction, which will only increase your darkness.

Addictive Behavior and Dark Energy

Our awareness is like a musical scale with many successive octaves. As we move up the scale from dark to light energy and from low to high vibration, or down from light to dark, we're really talking about shifting levels of consciousness. One thing that is always perceived as low vibration in an individual is any form of addiction, particularly excessive use of alcohol or drugs.

Using drugs such as marijuana, cocaine, and hallucinogens can affect the chakras negatively. So can prescription drugs, such as uppers and downers, painkillers, tranquilizers, antidepressants, and even certain diet pills if taken in quantities beyond those prescribed or for long periods of time. Drugs not only deaden your emotions, they can also artificially blow open a chakra, throwing you into a state of acute awareness for which your nervous system is unprepared, and then just as suddenly slam the chakra shut when the effects have worn off. Many people are too sensitive to handle either of these extremes, and their chakras remain stuck, either too open or totally closed. Both states are undesirable and unhealthy, and they can lead to long-term damage of the nervous system.

People who are spiritually evolved, who have expanded their energy field through organic practices such as meditation and prayer, are sometimes able to go beyond the physical plane to other higher planes. There, one can meet beings of a higher vibration, like angels. However, those who are not spiritually oriented or practiced in contemplative techniques may also go beyond the earth plane through the use of drugs, but when they arrive there, they encounter dark beings like demons and devils instead of angels. Individuals who expand their fields by force, as with drug use, can blow a chakra open and thereby accidently open the door to other levels, permanently getting stuck in a very dark place. You never want to force open a chakra.

I experienced this firsthand when I was a young lawyer with my first assistant, Rose. She appealed to me at the time because she could drink as much as I could. Alcohol is a depressant, and problem drinkers gravitate to one another so they don't feel bad about how much they're drinking. The practice seems innocuous and social when you're doing it together. I also knew that Rose favored cocaine, but I wasn't aware of how much she used, as it wasn't my drug of choice. When I gave up alcohol, I knew I would have to cease spending time with Rose. As a parting gift, I gave her what she had always wanted: a plane ticket to Alaska. (Addicts love to do "geographics," believing that life will be a lot better somewhere else.) She went to Alaska while I continued spending every evening at AA.

About three years later, I received an unexpected call from Rose. She was in town and needed to see me, because she had a serious legal problem that she said she couldn't talk about over the phone. We met on a beautiful sunny day at Lake Tahoe, where I still lived, and sat outside on a bench. Rose told me that she was being harassed at work in Alaska, and it was so extreme that her employers had told her to take a leave of absence to help her get beyond it. I kept asking who was doing the harassing, but she never quite explained it to me. Then, out of nowhere, she pointed up to the sky and said, "You see, there they are, the helicopters that follow me everywhere. That's who's harassing me!" I looked up and saw a pure blue sky with not a helicopter in sight. I suddenly realized that Rose had become paranoid from too much cocaine and alcohol, and that her mind was damaged. I found this incredibly frightening, depressing, and dark. I told her that she needed medical, not legal, attention and tried fruitlessly to get her to a 12-step program. Rose was not yet 30 years old.

You don't need any kind of advanced sensing abilities to know that your mother who drinks too much or your son who smokes weed every chance he gets has a low vibration; you've already recognized that. As you begin to learn how self-awareness heals, it starts to make sense to avoid the things that limit your own. All addictive behavior is, by its very nature, designed to keep us unaware. It's a Band-Aid, a coping mechanism. Whether the addiction is to drugs, alcohol, shopping, gambling, sex, cigarettes, eating—whatever it may be—we use it to avoid our feelings. We don't want to feel, we don't want to know, we don't want to be aware; it's just too painful.

I encourage you to turn the spotlight on your own darkness and work through what you find. The point is to bring your real feelings to your awareness, give them a voice, and acknowledge them. Take an honest look at what you're trying to avoid through your addictive behavior. To find the source of any darkness you may be fighting, and then release it, is one of the most powerful things you can do to move into greater light and joy.

For some, addictive behavior or other forms of escapism from inner darkness can lead to such large holes in their energy field that dark forces from the outside can get in and grab hold. Next, we'll look at the most terrifying of those possibilities: possession.

CHAPTER TWO

POSSESSED BY DARKNESS

"Dare to reach out your hand into the darkness,
to pull another hand into the light."

— NORMAN B. RICE

We all make deals with the dark, but when we make major ones—those that are serious and have the potential to destroy people's lives—we can invite the worst kind of darkness there is: an element of possession. This happens when our level of darkness becomes so great that we attract forces that can actually take us over, the way the man I met in France was possessed by an evil being of some kind.

Do these entities really exist? Yes, they do. And they always have. The oldest written reference to demonic possession comes from the Sumerians. Many of their tablets contain prayers to the gods, some looking for protection from demons and others asking for the demons that invaded their bodies to be cast out. In ancient Egypt and Babylonia, afflictions were attributed to evil spirits that invaded humans, and the healers carried out ceremonies to force darkness to depart. And virtually all shamanic cultures have priests who enter a trance state to rid a person of a disease that has come from a vengeful spirit, possibly an entity that was wronged by the individual needing the exorcism.

Jewish folklore and the teachings of the Kabbalah call an evil spirit a *dybbuk,* which is the soul of a dead person that enters someone's body to take care of unfinished business. It is released through an exorcism, which includes calling the names of the good angels. Jewish exorcism is done not only to drive away the dybbuk, but also to help both the possessor and the possessed in an act of healing.

In Islam, a *jinn* is an evil spirit and servant of Satan that can enter the human body and cause all sorts of grief, from illness to pain and torment. It can be expelled by reciting certain passages of the Koran.

In Hinduism, the Vedas talk about an evil spirit that can harm humans and even rebuff the will of the gods. Their exorcism rites include burning incense, prayer, sprinkling water from the holy rivers, blowing into conches, and offering sweets to the gods.

The most prominent examples of possession and exorcism arguably come from Christianity. In the New Testament, there are multiple references to Jesus driving out demons—the entities responsible for mental and physical disease. Jesus directly addressed the dark forces, not their victims. He described to his disciples how these beings acted when cast out, and taught the reasons behind their failures at exorcism. He gave express powers to the Apostles to cast out unclean spirits, warning the disciples against taking pride in the fact that the demons were subject to them. And before his ascension, he said, "In my name they shall cast out devils . . ." (Mark 16:17).

Hollywood has given us vivid pictures of modern-day priests who, in the name of Jesus Christ, battle the forces of darkness in possessed people. Exorcisms do happen in reality, even at the highest level of religious institutions. Pope John Paul II performed one on a woman in 1982, for example. It has also been said that Mother Teresa underwent an exorcism shortly before her death in 1997, because the Archbishop of Calcutta believed she was being assaulted by the devil.

Our present-day perspective, based on science, often views possession as mental illness. Diseases of the mind—schizophrenia, Tourette's syndrome, and certain forms of psychosis such as dissociative identity disorder (multiple personalities), for instance—can often be alleviated with medication, not with a cross and holy water. In the past, those who were mentally ill were often subjected to exorcisms that didn't work, and they were seen as evil. Nowadays, we've gone to the opposite extreme, believing that all evil is mental illness. It is not.

Schizophrenia or Possession?

At a recent workshop, a man came up to me during a break and asked, "Could you help my wife?"

He was one of many people who had approached me that day, but when I looked at him something prompted me to say, "Tell me about your wife."

"The doctors say she has schizophrenia," he replied. Schizophrenia is a very challenging problem for a healer to work on, let alone to teach others how to handle. The individual may be living in an imaginary world— hearing voices and feeling persecuted. Yet knowing that it was a rare opportunity for my students, I jumped at the chance to work with this woman.

Later in the afternoon, when the man's wife walked toward the stage, I could see from 30 feet away that she was 100 percent possessed, not schizophrenic. I became extremely careful as she approached, making sure not to look into her eyes so that I wouldn't confront the evil presence within her head-on. Possession is tricky, and I could very well have gotten hurt. I learned later that for much of the morning this woman had been writhing in her seat in the back row, making all kinds of sounds and motions, frightening the people around her.

Once the woman was onstage, I stood slightly behind her, out of her direct view, and spoke to her, delicately probing. She was still bobbing and weaving and acting very odd. The more I aimed the light at her, the more uncomfortable the situation became. As I was coaxing her to allow the energy that had just risen to her throat to leave her body, I kept saying, "Open your mouth. The energy is trying to leave. Just let the sound out." But instead of opening her mouth, she clamped her jaw tightly shut, obviously making a choice to refuse treatment. Ultimately, she went back to her seat and continued to act in a bizarre way.

It's important to remember that we're never possessed beyond our own willpower. This woman, while not happy about being ill (and on one level wanting to be healed), had formed a pact with the dark side and was gaining something from the arrangement, whatever that might have been. At a deep soul level, she made this choice and, when offered the opportunity to free herself of possession, didn't want to give it up. In other words, we can't help people who don't want assistance. We make deals with the devil all the time, and sometimes we have to pay with part of our soul. There's always going to be a price.

Compare this last example to a woman I met in Germany who took the stage and pleaded with me to release her from what she believed to be a case of possession. This instance was even sadder, because when I felt into her, I knew that her doctors had correctly diagnosed her with schizophrenia. In her case, I did a bit of delicate brain work to help untangle what felt like a mass of confused wiring, and then urged her to go to her physicians and resume taking the medication that could relieve her of the voices she was incessantly hearing. This was an excellent example of how the wisdom of conventional medicine and its pharmacopeia can assist someone who is in anguish. It also reminded me that sometimes the most critical thing I can do is help someone feel good about the surgery or medication that has been recommended to them; what they really need to hear is that having the procedure or taking the drugs is not a sign of weakness or defect. I know that particular woman left the workshop feeling tremendous relief about her future, no longer holding on to the self-punishing belief that she was somehow a failure because she required long-term medication.

Recognizing Possession

So how do you tell the difference between mental disease and possession, possibly in someone close to you? Well, there is a lot of gray area. Both the mentally ill and the possessed may be going through changes; for example, a shift in personality, perhaps swinging back and forth between manic and depressed behavior; a transformation in attitude and behavior, such as becoming more hostile; or obvious changes in personal hygiene. The individual may act increasingly abusive, destructive, or violent or have severe nightmares and hallucinations. Inappropriate emotional displays are also common in both. All of these symptoms can represent psychiatric or psychological changes, indicating Alzheimer's, drug abuse, or mental illness. Psychological intervention should be sought before considering the possibility of demonic possession, especially in teenagers.

A person may go through physical changes as well as mental ones, which can also have medical implications. For example, failure to blink the eyes for a long period of time can stem from a neurological condition, or someone might appear catatonic, which could be part of a mental illness. Changes in sleep patterns, sudden weight loss or gain, or other symptoms can have multiple causes.

However, some things that happen in cases of possession would be hard to label as psychiatric illness and can't be explained by neuroscience. A possessed person may exhibit outward manifestations, not just mental or physical changes. Objects may move around seemingly by themselves, disappear from one location and show up in another, or fly around as if thrown by unseen hands.

Knocking, banging, or pounding may be heard throughout a house or in a particular room. Doorbells may ring with no one present. Foul, acrid odors may come and go. Electrical appliances, lights, and gadgets may turn on or off. Animals may be spooked and stay away from the person or growl at something they sense but you do not. Sudden changes in temperature, a breeze when the windows are closed, or spontaneous fires may occur. There are many more possibilities as well.

Sometimes a person may be involved in the dark arts—the dark side of spirituality. They may even exhibit the same type of paranormal psychic powers that can manifest in a seeker of the light, such as having the ability to predict the future, speaking in tongues, or knowing what you are thinking.

There are, historically, certain telltale signs that, when seen together, can indicate demonic possession:

- Speaking or understanding languages that the person has never learned
- Revealing things that he or she has no earthly way of knowing
- Extraordinary demonstrations of strength beyond the individual's physical capabilities
- A violent aversion to spiritual things like holy water, a crucifix, or the name of God

Don't Try This at Home

Watching a *depossession*—also called an exorcism—can be deceiving: it looks much easier than it is. But they are extremely serious, and I treat them with the utmost caution. They require a great deal of personal energy on the part of the practitioner, in addition to the energy of the spirit guides that are called in to do the work.

Even though I may be in danger when trying to depossess someone at a workshop, my audience is not at risk. First, I put a template of protection over those who are present. Second, the possessing entity isn't interested in attacking anyone in the audience; it only wants to come after the person confronting it (me). In fact, the possessed individual can sometimes behave completely normally unless someone who's trained to address the dark energy walks into the room. Then, the entity will suddenly make itself obvious. That's because the more light that comes into the room, the more the darkness wants to make itself visible. While at some point the being may want to be transmuted by the light, that doesn't happen right away. Initially, it only wants to fight, and thus the age-old battle ensues between the dark and the light.

That's why I always tell my students, "Don't try this at home!" Never flirt with the idea of helping someone become disconnected from deep darkness. Leave it to the experts. I learned how to do this type of work mostly by watching and working with priests, ministers, and sha-mans who do exorcisms. I witnessed dozens upon dozens of depossessions before I ever attempted one, and it took me decades to acquire enough training to handle one by myself. It literally took me a lifetime to learn how to do this, and I treat it as if I'm dealing with an incredibly hot stove: I get the oven mitts. I get the fire extinguisher. I am supremely cautious, and I won't attempt it unless I'm certain I have the spiritual reinforcements to back me up.

When you witness enough exorcisms, you start to get a feel for the extent of the possession and the risk involved: *How strong is this one? How deeply is this person possessed? Is the darkness coming to the light, trying to be transmuted—or is it intent on taking me out now?* On many occasions, and for my own safety, I have removed myself quickly from the presence of a possessed person.

So, just to reiterate: *This is no joke. It's not a game, and it's definitely not something to try at home. As I said, if I'm not feeling strong enough, I won't even try it myself.*

One time as I was leaving the stage at the end of a large event, completely at the edge of exhaustion as I often am at that point, a woman walked right up to me and asked, "Can you help me?"

When I turned and looked in her eyes, I saw 100 percent possession. I replied to her as I looked away, "Whatever it is that you're studying, you need to dissociate yourself from it; it is incredibly dangerous for you."

She replied, "Oh, I know that now. It's a man I've been studying with in Paris." Then she repeated, "Can you help me?" I knew there was no way I could do it; I simply wasn't strong enough at that moment.

"I'm really sorry," I said, as I exited the room as fast as I could.

Unlike so many areas of my life, this is one place where I don't take any chances or risks. I have seen well-known, experienced exorcists lose control of situations, get overtaken, and then become unstable or ill themselves. Therefore, I always err on the side of caution.

You may be curious to know why it is that entities tend to show up at the end of long workshops when my strength is spent and I'm on the brink of exhaustion. I do have a theory, and it isn't what you might think—that the entities sense my weakness and come forward at a point when they'll have the greatest advantage. It's actually quite the opposite. It's my guides—those beings of light who work with me to do the healing—who are orchestrating the timing and prompting the possessed individuals to come forward for help at these particular moments. My guides want me at my lowest point to make sure that I'm totally "out of the way," meaning that I'll do my highest and best work when I'm not thinking about myself.

This expression and idea isn't exclusive to the healing world. A lawyer, for example, might make his best argument to the jury when his energy is totally depleted and he's only thinking about his client's highest good and what the jury needs to hear. Beyond fatigued, he has forgotten all about himself—about his own insecurities, doubts, and fears. I think that's why my guides bring me these tests when I'm at the brink of exhaustion in the last stages of my workshops. Since I can be truly out of the way in these moments, I can focus on doing the work as effectively as possible in order to get rid of the entity, end the session, and get some rest!

The Camel's Nose

Demons don't walk up to you and ask politely, "Hey! Do you want to be possessed?" as if you'd meekly nod your head and say, "Sure! Come right in." Instead, they find a weakness in your energy field, such as the place where you're attached to your family lineage of iniquities—the "sins of the fathers"—or your own reckless, addictive, or self-centered behavior. It's like the old story of the camel poking its nose into the tent: It starts with just the nose, and then before you know it the whole camel is inside. All it needs is an opening.

Let's say that you're in a relationship but find yourself responding to suggestive glances from one of your co-workers. Suddenly, you want to be with this person, even more than with your partner; and before you know it, you're having an affair. You never meant to cheat in thought, word, or—God forbid—deed, and certainly not with one of your co-workers . . . and yet you did. Now your life is a mess. You're lying to your partner and worrying that your boss will find out what's going on. Your emotions are in constant upheaval, yet you can't stop. All you can think about is your next encounter, and it's become an addiction. Others at work are starting to talk about how different you seem—distracted, laughing inappropriately, talking too much. If you're not careful, you'll lose your job and destroy your relationship. How could this be happening to you?

Understand that the gate that was breached, the one to the lower self, opens through the five senses: sight, smell, sound, taste, and touch. Darkness only needs an opening, a way to seduce the guardian at the door. The camel poked its nose into the tent, and you invited it in. Now there's very little room left for *you*, the real you. If you don't do something positive, something that ebbs the inflow of darkness and brings in more light—say, breaking it off with your co-worker and making amends with your partner—you may bring even greater darkness into your life.

Giving the Devil His Due

Since a fundamental part of our nature is that we are always striving to heal, always working toward whole-ness, always on a path of evolution and self-realization, it makes sense that what is dark at some point seeks to be brought into the light. To "give the devil his due," it is our darkness that eventually turns us to the light. But until it's ready to be transmuted, it desires to stay firmly planted in the unconscious and, therefore, will put up a real fight. However, when darkness is engulfed in a sea of light, as it will be when in the presence of higher con-sciousness, it's drawn out into the open to be released.

These days, this is why I'm seeing darkness a little more often at my workshops than in the past. The level of consciousness of the workshop participants (both those physically present as well as those attending via Livestream) keeps being raised as they initiate to more advanced levels while we're together. The higher in con-sciousness we go, the greater the likelihood of further expansion of our energy field, where more of our higher-self qualities get downloaded into our energy field and personality. These spiritual step-ups are called *initiations* in the West and *kundalini awakenings* in the East.

There are times when I look out from the stage and observe only a sea of bright light, and then there are times when dark areas stand out in the crowd. As you've seen in the examples I've shared, those people who are challenged with darkness often come forward during the course of the event to ask for assistance.

Many individuals are only mildly possessed by the dark, as in the case of my Chinese-American student Lin Lin. But some are fully possessed, like the woman whom I fled from without helping. There are also the participants who are clinically ill and not possessed at all, as in the case of the schizophrenic lady in Germany; it takes considerable intuition and training to be able tell the difference. The rest are garden-variety mixtures of light and dark, where the level of darkness is continually changing based on experiences and choices.

I remember back when I was a young lawyer and I turned to a fellow attorney one day and said, "This work is killing me." Incidentally, I had just won a big case and made a huge sum of money—enough, in fact, to be able to take a few years off.

"Killing you? You mean from the stress?" he asked.

"No," I answered. "It's because I'm doing my job from a place of not being true to myself." There was something about my work that I knew wasn't right; it wasn't coming from a place of sanctity or good intent. I didn't seem to be able to practice law from a wholesome place. Rather, I would always attack the opposition mercilessly; I had to win at all costs.

I want to make it clear that the law itself wasn't the problem; the problem was me. It is possible to practice law, or engage in any other kind of endeavor, with a high degree of integrity. In fact, my father, who certainly had his dark side, was an extremely ethical attorney. But at that time, I would walk a fine line and even step over it in order to win a case. The realization that I wasn't coming from an enlightened standpoint prompted me to leave that profession and change the course of my life. The need to win was just too prevalent in me, and the only way I could cure it was to withdraw from that world and humble myself. So I became a menial assistant to other healers—a position I stayed in for many years. This decision was a crucial turning point for me that set me on the course of bringing in far more light.

And that's where we're headed next. We'll leave the darkness for a while now and begin to explore the highest vibration there is—the light.

CHAPTER THREE

Let There Be Light

"From within or from behind, a light shines through us upon things and makes us aware that we are nothing, but the light is all."

— Ralph Waldo Emerson

The energy that brought us to life also brought the universe to life. We all ride atop an underlying intelligence that surrounds and permeates everything in existence—an energy that is All That Is. We come from it, we're connected to it, and each one of us is its living expression. Some people call it God, some call it Source, and some call it the light.

When discussing energy healing, I've used the term *unified field* from the world of physics—but really, this is love. The basic energy of the universe is unconditional love, and it is the strongest force there is. Plain and simple, tapping into it is a remedy on this physical plane for our hearts, minds, and bodies. Its capacity for healing supersedes the physical laws of nature, because it created nature and is much grander than the limitations of the material world. As such, it is in fact the stuff that miracles are made of.

Connecting to higher-vibration energy is your birthright. It's what your soul—having come from the light—longs to do. The ability to harness this energy is part of who you are as a being on this planet. It's in your energetic structure, your physiology, your DNA. It's also always present for you, accessible and waiting. It rejoices in your connection to it and passes on its blissful feeling to you the moment that bond is formed.

Since our souls want to experience the light, and since the goal of the soul is to return to the higher consciousness it knew before arriving here, participating in activities that connect us to the light is nourishing for our souls. It's like coming home after a very long time of being away.

So how do you connect? Even though this energy is everywhere at all times, it does come through in greater strength and intensity in particular places, in the presence of certain people, at certain times, and through specific spiritual practices such as meditation and prayer.

High-Energy Places

As the ancients knew, some places on Earth are graced with high-vibration energy. Wise and intuitive people often built their holiest institutions over energy vortexes. They knew that bathing in these elevated vibrations was beneficial to raising their consciousness and facilitated their spiritual development. There are numerous such power places around the world, and you don't have to be highly sensitive to feel them. Haven't you ever walked into a church or cathedral and felt something extraordinary? Or visited one of the mysterious sites like Stonehenge and felt the power of the place?

When you arrive at one of these sacred sites, you may very well feel the kind of shift in energy I'm describing. Each place will most likely feel different from the others, but they all feel different from the rest of the world. When you stand on the main plaza at Machu Picchu, surrounded by the towering peaks of the Andes; gaze up at the mighty pyramids of Egypt; or visit the ancient holy cities of Banaras or Jerusalem or Mecca, each lets you know in its own way that you are on sacred ground.

Building Over Pagan Sites

One of my favorite activities whenever I travel is to visit the local church or cathedral in the town I'm staying in and sense the energy there. Sometimes it's incredibly high, often because the structure was built over the site where the area's pre-Christian pagans held their services, rituals, and meetings. What the Christians didn't realize was that the natives already knew it was a holy place, which is why their shrines and temples were located there.

Chartres, just outside Paris, France, is a wonderful example of a cathedral constructed above an extremely powerful vortex. The site was a place of pilgrimage long before the cathedral was built, as people traveled to the Druidic sanctuary of Gaul—the grotto in Chartres, which later became the crypt of the cathedral. Most Druidic goddess sanctuaries had a sacred well, and the one at Chartres is still visible today, although it is now dry. When it became Christianized, it was named Saints-Forts—which loosely translates to "Well of the Holy Strong Ones"—after the first martyrs were drowned in it. You can't miss the high energy of this site the moment you step foot in the cathedral. You know you are on holy ground.

Many Christian churches were built on sites specifically to replace pagan shrines, as part of the Roman imperial policy to eradicate the "unholy" pagan gods and goddesses, especially in the land of the Bible. The Church of the Nativity in Bethlehem replaced a shrine dedicated to the god of agriculture, Tammuz-Adonis. The Church of the Holy Sepulchre, which supposedly marks the site of the crucifixion and burial of Jesus, replaced a temple to Venus, the goddess of sex and fertility. Constantine personally ordered the tearing down of the Temple of Venus so he could erect a church in honor of the Holy Cross, his personal battle emblem. Another important pagan site was the Temple of Aphrodite at Ein Karim near Jerusalem, which was torn down and replaced by a church dedicated to the birth of St. John the Baptist.

The destruction of the holy shrines and temples of the pre-Christian era couldn't destroy the inherent power of these sites. Instead, one can imagine a spiritual archeological dig, with one religion's structures replacing the previous ones, going down through time until the original natural vortex of high energy is revealed.

Visiting Sacred Sites

When I was in Munich holding a workshop, someone said, "Oh, you're really going to want to see this local country church; it has a great feeling." So my host drove me all the way to the site, two hours outside the city. It was well worth the time. The moment I stepped into the church, I could feel its high vibration. The structure was old and had been built on a hill overlooking a beautiful lake. My guess is that the local inhabitants erected it there because their predecessors knew from the indigenous people before them that this was a sacred location. It clearly had a special energetic feel to it, much as Sedona, Arizona, does.

In fact, one of the very first experiences I ever had with a high-energy place happened when I was first in Sedona. As mountain climbers, my husband and I were interested in scaling the area's famous Red Rocks. To us, it sounded like a great place for climbing—we had no idea that it was also heralded as a location of strong spiritual energy.

Eric and I pulled into Sedona with a carful of climbing gear and our mountain bikes mounted on the back. Eager to do some biking, we stopped at a spot that looked like a nice place to ride. It was a beautiful area, with amazing, towering red cliffs. We got on our bikes and rode for a long time, getting farther from town. All of a sudden, we saw quite a few bikes lying at the bottom of a hill. Curious, we parked there, too, and headed up the hill on foot, as we presumed the other riders had done. At the top were dozens of people sitting on the ground in the middle of a geometric design. I didn't know what a mandala was back then, but everyone was meditating.

We like to meditate, I thought excitedly. *Let's join them!* So we sat down on the ground, cross-legged, at the outer edge of the group and meditated for about an hour. A few minutes into it, I could tell that the area was especially conducive to deep meditation.

Once we were done, my husband and I walked down the hill, got back on our bikes, and headed to the car. That's when it struck me that I had undergone a major transformation. As we made our way toward the car, it seemed as if I were flying! I couldn't get over how light I felt. Taken aback, I kept trying to figure it out. *What is it that happened to me up there on that hill? Why am I so filled with this buoyant energy that I don't even need a bike? I could run above the street if I wanted!* It was an extraordinarily, uplifting feeling, and it lasted a couple of hours before eventually wearing off.

Back at the hotel, still intrigued, I bought an armful of books and started reading all about Sedona. I learned that it is known for being a very special, incredibly energetic place, as it's located over a vortex, a place of spiraling spiritual energy on multiple dimensions, often including water. The Native Americans have always known about it; in fact, there are all kinds of petroglyphs and other evidence of ancient life in the area. And many people, not as ignorant about it as I was back then, continue to go there in droves to experience the unusual energy.

Pilgrimage

A pilgrimage to a sacred site is a wonderful way to connect to the light. Take a moment now to imagine where you might like to go to experience it in a different way from your usual routine. To that end, one of my friends went on a pilgrimage to a small island called Putuoshan off the east coast of China; it has been sacred to Kuan Yin, the Buddhist bodhisattva (goddess) of compassion, for over 4,000 years. Even decades of "godless" Communism couldn't erase the sacredness of the island, which had formerly been home to thousands of Chinese Buddhist monks and nuns who were devoted to the goddess. Many temples are now being rebuilt, and a statue of Kuan Yin the size of the Statue of Liberty overlooks the South China Sea.

But you don't have to travel halfway around the world to connect to a sacred site. North America is brimming with places that were held sacred by Native Americans for thousands of years. Do some research in your local area, and I'm certain you will come across some surprises. My personal favorite is an oasis and spa outside Tucson at the foot of the Santa Catalina Mountains called Miraval. There is no way to quantify the intense spiritual energy I experience there. I've worked with hundreds of students in workshops at Miraval and have noticed after they've been there a few days that their root chakra, the one that connects them to Mother Earth and the health of their body, becomes much larger and more powerful. I've named this phenomenon "the Miraval effect."

Connecting to the Light at a Special Time

There are certain times when the light is stronger than usual. For example, in India there are mass pilgrimages, tens of millions of people strong, called Kumbha Melas. During these events, spiritual seekers gather at certain locations because bathing in the holy rivers at the correct astrological moment—calculated according to a special combination of the positions in the zodiac of the sun, moon, and Jupiter—will purify the bathers from their karmic debts. These events take place in four different locations on holy rivers once every 12 years.

Every year on the summer solstice, thousands of people gather just before daybreak at Stonehenge in southern England. It is on that date that the massive stones are aligned almost perfectly with the sunrise. Most ancient sacred sites, in fact, are aligned with particular moments in time. The Intihuatana stone at Machu Picchu is positioned to point directly at the sun during the winter solstice, as is the entrance to Newgrange, the prehistoric monument in Ireland where the sun travels down the passage tomb only on the winter solstice to illuminate the inner chamber for 17 minutes. The Mayan temple of Kukulcán at Chichen Itza in the Yucatán, Mexico, puts on a brief but amazing show at sunset on the vernal and autumnal equinoxes: the sun's light and the edges of the stepped terraces on the pyramid create a shadow display on the sides of the northern stairway, which gives the impression of a long tail heading down to the stone head of the serpent Kukulcán at the base of the stairs. There, a doorway leads to an inner staircase that ends in a small, mysterious shrine. Thousands of pilgrims believe it to be a particularly auspicious time.

There may also be a best time of life in which to focus on activities and practices that lead you into more light. In the classical teachings of India, four stages of life are delineated: the student, the householder, the hermit, and the wandering ascetic. In the hermit stage, when householder duties come to end, a believing Hindu who is not a monk or a saint, but has a family, a job, a home, and worldly possessions, would begin the shift of giving up everything that belongs to the small self. He no longer wants the complications that distract him from what needs to be done, which is connecting to Spirit and doing good works. The last stage is that of *sannyasi*—the ascetic who is totally devoted to God with no home and no attachments, with the sole goal of attaining liberation. Although few people follow these stages in this day and age, the urge to simplify and turn toward Source becomes a strong pull for many at any time of life.

Becoming an Ascetic

My father-in-law, Hubert, a French businessman and artist, was a shining example of the spiritual resurgence that can happen toward the end of life. During his last ten years, he changed rather dramatically by becoming an ascetic.

After 65 years of marriage, Hubert's wife passed away. My in-laws had already sold their magnificent summerhouse, their apartment in Cannes, and their grand apartment in Grenoble. In the European tradition, they had lived frugally on the proceeds, never adopting the more extravagant, spendthrift American ways. Then, not wanting to be encumbered by possessions in his final years, Hubert gave away the last few things he owned: his artwork—beautiful watercolors and sculptures—and his furniture. He moved into a monastic setting, a home for retired priests. He even gave up the Catholic guilt that had caused him so much unhappiness in life. His prolific letters, always poetic and philosophical, became even more focused on the meaning of life.

Hubert also became more real in the years leading up to his death. The courtly manners that were so much a part of his demeanor, which had often disguised his emotions, no longer hid the way he felt. Rather than medicate himself in his final stage, as so many are inclined to do, he stayed as aware as possible, even after he fell off his bike at age 90 and needed a hip replacement. He cheerfully spoke of being ready to die and did so just a few hours shy of his 95th birthday. My father-in-law, like a good Indian householder, heeded the inner call to simplify and focus on what was really important.

"Enlightened" People

In addition to special places and times, certain people exhibit especially high concentrations of the light. This means that their vibration, which equates to their consciousness, is very high. We typically refer to these spiritually aware individuals as enlightened beings. Saints, seers, and healers throughout history have accessed the light for Divine knowledge or to transmit its energy through their own energy field to share with others. We often see them portrayed in artwork with halos surrounding their heads, indicating that their personal energy field has amassed a great deal of light.

In every tradition you'll find revered masters, teachers, and leaders who have exhibited extraordinary wisdom and abilities that come from their immense connection to the light.

If you find that enlightened beings from a particular tradition call to you—whether they are from your own or another that you're drawn to—you can place a picture of them in your home and start a conversation. Unlike others who have departed from this world and moved on to other adventures, these beings opted not to go "off the grid," so to speak. They have stayed nearby to be of service to humanity and are ready to help you step more into the light.

The Christ Light

One of the most light-filled persons known to have walked the planet was the man named Jesus. I say "the man," because I believe he was a man and not a god. He was one of the enlightened or ascended masters with a mission to touch millions upon millions of people throughout the last 2,000 years. There are other fully enlightened beings who radiated their light and spread a high vibration but did not have a mission to teach or heal. They may have simply sat in a cave high in the Himalayas and blessed the world in that way.

I look to Jesus because of the astonishing feats he performed using the light, which was most pronounced in his ability to cure the sick. He could open his heart chakra fully, all 360 degrees, and direct a huge amount of energy to others. In doing so, he assisted individuals at both the physical and the soul levels, including healing huge groups at the same time. This highly evolved level of consciousness is often referred to as the *Christ light.* Jesus himself said, "I am the Light of the world. No follower of mine shall wander in the dark; he shall have the light of life."

The Divine Feminine

When a woman is a fully enlightened being, it is said that she embodies the Divine Feminine, which is another aspect of unconditional love. This archetypal energy has been embodied many times throughout the ages—including as Kuan Yin, the Buddhist goddess of compassion; Isis, the Egyptian goddess of healing; and later as Jesus's mother, the Virgin Mary, both in her actual lifetime 2,000 years ago and in her many subsequent visitations, such as Our Lady of Lourdes, Our Lady of Fátima, Our Lady of Guadalupe, and the Black Madonna statues and paintings that have been associated with healings and other miracles attributed to her energy. There are additional sites of Marian apparitions around the globe, Medjugorje in Bosnia and Herzegovina for one, that continue to receive millions of visitors each year who come with the expectation of experiencing healing miracles. These spots are high-energy places both because of the light Mary's visitations bring and the passionate energy of the faithful in attendance.

Mother Mary, then, is one face of the Divine Feminine. Another incarnation of this archetype is Mary Magdalene, whom I believe was a disciple of Jesus and likely his most gifted follower. Because she was a woman in a patriarchal time, I suspect she was pushed out after Jesus's death by some of his other disciples and followers.

Kuan Yin, known as the goddess of mercy and compassion, is an Eastern manifestation of the Divine Mother. She serves humankind in much the same way as Mother Mary and is sometimes referred to as the Buddhist Madonna. Her title and office as a goddess simply mean that she has attained the level of a cosmic being. In Japan, she is known as Kannon, and in China her name is Guanyin. For Tibetan Buddhists, she is called Tara. The story goes that Kuan Yin paused on the threshold of heaven because she heard the cries of the world. She turned back and vowed to help those in need on Earth, however long that might take, which is really the definition of the bodhisattva vow.

Another of the female ascended masters is Lady Master Nada. In this case, the word *nada* means the "voice of the silence," which gives way to the Christ Self. One of her services to humankind is directing healing to those of us on Earth. In one of her incarnations here, Lady Nada served as a priestess in the Temple of Love on Atlantis. In another, she took up the law and became an expert in the defense of those who were oppressed. She saw the law as the best defense a mother could use to protect her children from those "fallen ones" who used the law for unjust purposes.

Initiation—an Infusion of Light

One of the ways to connect to more light within yourself is to be in the presence of someone who holds more light than you do—an individual with a higher vibration than yours. This is why people look to teachers, gurus, and others who promise enlightenment to seekers. Because of the law of resonance, there is great benefit to being around a spiritual mentor who is connected to Source, since he or she acts as a magnet for higher energies. By being around that person, your energy field is positively affected. This is the meaning of the "guru effect" and the reason people want to sit at the feet of those who have achieved an advanced level of enlightenment, or light.

Some teachers are particularly gifted at bringing in uplifting energies for others. In other words, they have an innate talent for facilitating initiations. When you have done the needed inner work and are ready to receive the energy from your eighth and higher chakras, such a guide can act as a midwife, helping to download that expanded energy into you. Keep in mind, though, that an initiation only gets offered to those who are ready, and not before.

If you're regularly engaged in self-examination and have achieved enough self-awareness to transform your personal darkness, *and* I can pick up that you've got a strong base of meditation and/or prayer, I can raise you up from one level to another. The caveat here is that I've got to sense that foundation or it won't be safe for you. Much in the same way as the earlier discussion about drugs, being pulled up prematurely can really hurt you. On top of that, it can be devastating because when you reach a level you aren't prepared for and are unable to hold that level, it can deprive you of ever attaining it again in this lifetime. It's also possible, of course, to lose an initiation through excess pride, the nemesis of every aspirant. Sometimes I'll sense that an individual wishes for an initiation, but he or she doesn't have the spiritual base of meditation or prayer that's required to support it. I may say to this person, "Go home, meditate for a few months, and then come see me again; perhaps we'll make it happen at that point."

My student Veronica was a good example of this. For years she'd been longing for an initiation, but it just never happened. The higher energies were not coming in for her, and she was becoming impatient and frustrated. At one workshop, she finally said, "I give up," and she sincerely let go of trying to make it happen. It was only after Veronica forgot all about it that I happened to look at her from across the room. She was busily working at a table in the back, helping one of the attendees with something, when I saw the initiatory energy just above her head. Finally, it was her moment! I dropped everything and rushed over to help bring it in.

"But I Don't Meditate"

One of the more interesting initiations I've facilitated happened at an apprentice workshop to a man named Roger. At certain points over the weekend, I had the attendees take turns practicing on each other while I led them through different healing techniques. That's how Roger came to my attention.

During a question-and-answer session following one of the practice times, a woman raised her hand and said that she'd experienced the most amazing transformation. I looked at her and could see that her energy field was expanded. "Who have you worked with today?" I asked. Since participants had each partnered with two different people so far, I added, "Let's have the two people who worked with this gal please stand." A man and a woman from the audience stood up. A quick glance told me it was the man who had created the shift, as his field was radiant. "Why don't you come up here?" I requested from the stage. As he started to approach, another woman jumped up and exclaimed, "He worked on me, too, and I also feel changed!" I looked at her and became even more interested in this man.

The moment Roger walked up to me, he started to have a major initiation. Once I helped bring the energy in, I said to him, "Stay up here with me; you're ready to help others." Immediately, I could sense his hesitation, as if he were afraid that I'd find him out and reveal him as a fraud. At least, that's what he was thinking. He whispered, "I need to tell you, I've never meditated a day in my life."

I looked at him discerningly. "Well, for a guy who's never meditated, you've got some form of amazing practice. You *are* connecting to Source, and it feels like it's on a daily basis. I'm sensing that it's through nature. Are you out in nature a lot?"

"I'm in the Coast Guard," he replied. "A captain."

"That explains it. You're one with the ocean."

"You're right, I am," he said as tears welled up in his eyes. "But they won't let me work anymore." Roger went on to explain that, after a car accident, he had undergone spinal surgery where he had been given too much anesthetic, which damaged his heart. The doctors told him the problem was irreversible and he didn't have much time left to live. He certainly wasn't being allowed to captain any ships given that he was at risk of suddenly keeling over.

"I still live right next to the ocean. I go there every day to walk and breathe it in," he told me.

"Well, you've got a natural healing gift here," I said. "This right turn in your life, this 180-degree about-face, has brought you to what you're meant to do, which is healing work. Welcome to the club! No, you won't be piloting any more ships. *This* is what you're going to be doing, so let me show you how." I had him work on a few more people on the stage while I showed him how to use his own, as well as universal, energy to make healing happen.

Cultivating the Light Through Meditation

So why do some people have so much more light than others? Frankly, it depends on how much they've worked at cultivating it. While we all have issues—our own personal darkness—we don't all work at resolving them. Not everyone focuses on connecting to the light. How much light we have is a direct reflection of the inner work we've done.

If you're curious to know how much light you have, ask yourself how hard you work at really getting to know yourself. Do you make no effort, living in your lower self and using alcohol, drugs, or other escapist behaviors when you don't feel well? Do your negative habits and mind-sets cause you to reside in drama, self-pity, or bitterness; damage your relationships through resentment or narcissism; or blame others when life doesn't go your way? Or are you actively striving to be encouraging and uplifting and to give more? Besides working through your problems, are you regularly connecting with Source, with the light? Are you being of service in some way, no matter how small?

Keep in mind that we can prepare ourselves for further enlightenment with the practice of meditation. To release our inner darkness and bring in more light, we need information. We must root out the true cause of what's ailing us and find the most expeditious and effective path for releasing it—I certainly learned this when I had cancer, yet the wisdom and insights that come after (not during) meditation assist us in healing every area of our lives. On an energetic level, this practice helps us remove any blockages that come from holding on to anger and resentment, from harboring shame and self-blame. Meditation thereby ushers in the most crucial part of the healing process: self-forgiveness. It opens us to our connections to ourselves, other people, and All That Is. In this way, it also paves the way for global harmony and peace.

By expanding your awareness—by bringing yourself into balance, experiencing greater peace, raising your consciousness, and connecting with the Divine light—you are actually assisting every other person and creature on the planet to do the same. We're all connected by one vast field of energy. The ripples that you send out into the world are reflections of your inner state of being; they touch and affect others. If you're uplifted, you uplift others. If all human beings are in a higher state, we'll very likely feel more inclined to come to creative and harmonious solutions to our global problems. That's what enhanced consciousness is going to give us: a world without war, terrorism, rapacious bankers, polluted air, or toxic water. Simply put, it can bring about a better life for us all. The most important reason to meditate, then, is to heal not just ourselves but also the planet.

All beings on Earth communicate with one another through consciousness. That's why what you think and feel is so important—with every thought and emotion you have, you're sending out a wave of energy that makes its way into the fabric of humanity's consciousness. If enough people send out the same thoughts and feelings on a particular topic, the cultural or even world belief about that subject will change.

Look, for example, at the number of individuals who now approve of same-sex relationships because of their exposure to hit shows like *Modern Family* and *Glee*, which make ordinary viewers feel comfortable with gay marriage. As a result, there is much less objection to it. Gay and lesbian relationships soon will be as ordinary as women voting, as it should be. That's how the collective consciousness works; we share ideas. We go to bed at night having watched a documentary about Chaz Bono, which prompts us to begin to understand his plight of feeling like a man in a woman's body, and the next day we feel differently about transgender issues now that we've been exposed to the idea. Eventually, compassion and acceptance become more prominent than negative views.

This is one reason I have my students meditate together at workshops: our state of mind produces waves of energy that don't just affect the people in the group or our next-door neighbors. The larger and more powerful the group, the farther the energy radiates, affecting those at greater distances. I discovered this earlier on, in one of my first major experiences with meditation when I went to study at the Maharishi's school.

The Maharishi's Meditation

Perhaps the most famous meditation teacher around the world was Maharishi Mahesh Yogi, the founder of Transcendental Meditation (TM). Although he is best known for becoming the spiritual advisor to the Beatles in 1967 and teaching them how to meditate, he was actually a simple monk who became inspired in 1959, when he was in his 40s, to bring meditation to the Western world. And that is exactly what the Maharishi did over the next few decades on his world tours.

I first heard of him in the '70s. He founded the Maharishi School of the Age of Enlightenment (MSAE) in 1974, where all college subjects were taught, along with meditation. My husband and I learned his basic meditation practice in California and then decided to go to the school in Fairfield, Iowa, and spend some time there. The moment we arrived, we found ourselves attracted to the place and ended up staying for a number of years.

The school was located about an hour and a half from the nearest airport in Cedar Rapids. Driving along the freeway in our rental car, the cornfields lining either side of the road higher than we could see from our windows, I already sensed the energy as we approached Fairfield. To me, the change was palpable; we could truly feel the school before we arrived because of the thousands of people who were gathered there to meditate. I found this to occur time and again when my husband and I traveled throughout India, Nepal, and similar areas, going from one ashram or holy shrine to another. Without fail, whenever we were within 20 to 30 miles, there was a noticeable shift in the energy. This is what happens when conscious individuals are proactively working on raising their vibration in a group setting.

While at the Maharishi's school, I had an extraordinary experience. One morning, we devotees were sitting on the cushions in total silence with our eyes closed, mentally hearing a powerful *sutra* (a short aphorism). All of sudden, I started to feel heat coming from my hands, up my arms, up my neck, and into my head. I remember thinking, *I'm too young to be having a hot flash.* Then I saw in my mind's eye an amazing vision of one body in the room, not 75; we were all so connected that we became one. I gasped in delight as I merged into this vision; I could feel one heart beating inside of me, and it contained the hearts of all the people in the room.

When the meditation ended, the head teacher called on me and asked if I'd share what I had just experienced. Later, when I was more trained, I realized that she had been able to perceive the higher-level initiation energies entering me with her advanced training, just as I can now observe them when they enter you. Chances are that the teacher could even sense the vision I had of the union of the group as one beating heart.

Connecting to the Light Through Prayer

There are probably a million different ways to connect to the light. Absolutely anything in the human experience can trigger this connection and spark joy. Some of the more common ways are activities where we are engaged in something larger than ourselves: for example, being in nature, sharing intimacies with a partner, giving birth, or being with a loved one when he or she dies. The two most consistent and reliable methods for connecting to the light and, more important, the ones that develop your ability to connect *at will,* are prayer and meditation.

Prayer is such an old-fashioned term that I hesitate to use it here. It sounds like something your mother, father, pastor, or rabbi told you to do many years ago—something you *should* do, like flossing your teeth or eating your vegetables. The thought of putting your palms together and getting down on bended knee might make you feel uncomfortable or even insincere.

Chances are that the idea of praying only crosses your mind if you have a serious problem that you feel incapable of resolving by yourself: you've just had a major relationship breakup, gotten news that you have a life-altering disease, or received word that a loved one has been in a terrible accident and may not survive. These are the kinds of extreme circumstances that inspired the old maxim, "There are no atheists in foxholes." You promise God or whoever else might be listening that if only He will change this event, you'll be a saint from this moment on. We use this form of prayer, called *petition,* to ask for things ranging from our rent money to a new love, house, or car . . . all the way up to world peace. We connect to Source to request something, but prayer can also involve not asking for anything.

When I was a small child, perhaps as young as three years old, I learned how to pray. I was taught through my Catholic upbringing to connect with the figures that are prominent in that faith: God the Father; his son, Jesus; and Jesus's parents, Mary and Joseph. I also knew about something more nebulous called the Holy Spirit, and about all the angels and saints. I was taught that if

I reached out to these figures in the spirit world, they would both listen to me and communicate in return. I learned to connect with them three or four times a day, and by the time I was about five, I not only spoke to these divine figures, but I heard them speaking back to me as well. In the insulated culture I was living in, made even more closed off by attending religious schools, I never doubted that these connections were real.

While I later abandoned these relationships during my teenage years and only returned to them after getting sick in my 20s, the foundation that was established early on gave me a special adeptness with the practice. Later, as I studied a variety of traditions for their secrets to healing, I connected to figures in other faiths as well. Nevertheless, I've found that I connect most effortlessly to the icons from my own background.

It may be easiest for you to start out by addressing the enlightened beings that you know about from your own background, if they appeal to you. If you didn't grow up in a faith tradition or are uncomfortable with the one you were raised in, by all means choose something else that works for you: ancestors, angels, or even your higher self—the god-self within you that's located above your head in your higher chakras. The bottom line is to use whatever you identify with and gives you the greatest sense of connectedness when you pray. And prayer doesn't have to involve words. At its heart, this practice is about joining to the light, Source, God, or whatever name you have for the energy of unconditional love.

Other Forms of Prayer

I actually have very unconventional ideas about what prayer can be. You're probably already familiar with affirmations, although you may not have thought of them as prayer. They are actually a step up energetically, because they engage the energy of Source in the *present* moment rather than the future. Petition, or prayer, oftentimes reflects wanting something you don't have: "God, please bring me a great-looking guy!" With affirmations, you're saying that you already have whatever it is you want: "I love my partner!" Picture in your mind whatever it is you are praying about—a more loving relationship, better health, more abundance—and know that it already exists, thus allowing Spirit to help you manifest it.

Another use of affirmations that's more relevant to increasing your light is to declare a shift into your higher-self qualities—those residing in your upper chakras. Do you want the gift of healing? State that this skill is already unfolding in you: "I am able to heal." Do you want to be an instrument of peace and love? Declare, "I am an instrument of peace and love." Of course, you must also take action on the physical plane to bring your desire to life. Once you have your vision solidly in mind and you state your affirmation, look for the most obvious next action to manifest that goal into reality. As the quote that's often attributed to Goethe goes, "What you can do, or dream you can do, begin it! Boldness has genius, power, and magic in it." Spirit helps those who help themselves.

We can also connect to the light through our creative activities, where our intention is simply to dance with the Divine. One way to do this is to offer ourselves up as channels, where we ask or intend that the light moves through us and out into the world via our talents and gifts. Another method is to consciously spend time communing with the light while doing activities such as dance, yoga, or Pilates; or through artistic endeavors such as writing, art, or music in which the activity—the dance, the piece of writing or art, or the music—becomes a co-creation between ourselves and Source. This is a profound way to connect and interact with the energy of the light.

Focused Intent

You can also connect to the light through a practice I call *focused intent*. Using this intent is along the same lines as stating an affirmation, but at a much higher intensity. The method involves concentrating on a desired end result with such magnitude that every fiber of your being, all the way down to your eyelashes, is yearning, even screaming, for connection and fulfillment. This is the kind of prayer that can cure the sick—literally. It's one of the primary techniques I teach in healing at the physical level.

So how do you *do* focused intent? Well, it's a bit difficult to describe in words and much easier to teach in action. What I have noticed is that the focused intention I used in the past to win a lawsuit, ride a horse impeccably through a series of dressage steps, or ski a perfect race was the same kind of focus I need nowadays to create healing. I have to make sure that every ounce of me is pointed in the same direction and at the same time to bring about a singular result. It's a laserlike concentration. Think, for example, about those individuals who have the gift of telekinesis, of affecting material objects using only their minds. That's the kind of focus I'm referring to—the type needed to bend a spoon or transport an object across a room without touching it. This is all about intentionality, creating a space for a particular thing to happen, and then seeing it and allowing it to occur with every fiber of your being.

Healing Using Focused Intent

In energy healing, I use focused intent to attract the light, transmit it through my own field, and then direct it to the person who needs to receive it. How does this transfer of light work? Think about the way so many of our everyday experiences involve energy traveling over long distances in short amounts of time, such as an e-mail crossing the ocean from one country to another in a matter of seconds. In this respect, it doesn't take much imagination to picture healing intent being faster than the speed of light.

Another perspective is that it's actually not necessary for the energy used in healing to travel anywhere. This is my sense of how things work: The whole is contained within every part of the universe. Therefore, there is no such thing as time or distance; these are only concepts that help us navigate our physical world. At the level of the unified field, of Source, we are all connected and able to affect one another. It's through our mutual attachment to this field that distance healing works. For this reason, we strive to access the unified field by going into an expanded state of awareness through practices such as prayer and meditation.

One Saturday afternoon at a workshop, in order to demonstrate distance healing, I asked for a volunteer from among the participants who were attending over the Internet via Livestream. A woman named Sally wrote in to our chat line to say that she was at home nursing a broken ankle after a mountain-biking accident and that she'd had surgery just the day before. She mentioned that she was a personal trainer and that the surgeon had told her she wouldn't be able to walk for three months. With her permission, I used her situation to demonstrate to the group how to do distance healing. I utilized my focused intent to picture this woman in my mind's eye in her natural state of perfection—completely well and enjoying herself riding a mountain bike. The session was quick and effortless. Afterward, I asked Sally how she felt. She immediately typed back to say that during the healing session the broken ankle had gotten very warm.

About a week later, she posted a YouTube video to say that she'd returned to her doctor for a checkup, and he had been shocked by her excellent progress and had declared that her anticipated healing time had been reduced from the original three months to just three weeks! Sally was thrilled. This is the power and excitement of energy healing that employs an advanced form of intentionality, which looks much like prayer. At times a complete, instantaneous recovery can be achieved or, as in Sally's case, it can be dramatically sped up and improved.

The light isn't limited in what it can do; we are only limited in knowing how to use it. Not long ago, I had a serious fall where I tore two major ligaments and fractured three bones in my knee. Unable to stand, I was told by the doctor that I needed immediate surgery or I'd never again walk without pain or a limp. I'd injured my other knee many years before in a mountain-climbing accident, which had required surgery that necessitated a long recovery. This time I wasn't interested in having an invasive procedure, but considering that I travel incessantly and stand for days on end to do my work, I was certainly eager to find a cure as quickly as possible.

For the first couple of weeks after the accident, I was on crutches and even used a wheelchair at times. I couldn't stand for more than a few minutes without being in excruciating pain and becoming exhausted. So when I had to teach a weekend workshop—where I'd have to stand for six to eight hours per day—just a few weeks after the accident, I thought I might have to teach sitting down, something I had never done and wasn't looking forward to. When the first day of the event arrived, I was thrilled to find that the moment I walked onstage for the first session on Friday night, I was able to stand—my knee was strong and pain free! Furthermore, I had no trouble remaining on my feet that night for the full two hours and on Saturday for the entire eight-hour day. The same thing happened on Sunday, too. As long as I held my focus on those who needed my help and stayed in the healing zone, everything was fine. The recovery was miraculous. Yet the moment the workshop ended on the final day and I left the room, my knee started to feel weak; and by the time I left the hotel a few hours later, I was back on crutches.

What I took from that experience was that while I knew how to conduct the healing energy through my body to a recipient, such as Sally, I hadn't quite figured out how to hold that force in my own body. Even those of us who are spiritual teachers have much to learn and, as you'll see in the next chapter, we're not always successful.

CHAPTER FOUR

FALLING FROM GRACE

"We can easily forgive a child who is afraid of the dark; the real tragedy of life is when men are afraid of the light."

— OFTEN ATTRIBUTED TO PLATO

As I mentioned previously, people and places that once were in the light can peak and lose power, or even slip into darkness. We can absolutely fall from grace. This happens more frequently than you might think. In fact, in my 30-plus years in this line of work—most of my adult life—I've often seen this occur. When I officially entered the spiritual world, I would hear glowing reviews of gurus, seers, or saints, but when I visited them, they wouldn't be anything like the tales I'd heard. Not only were they unholy and lacking saintly qualities, sometimes they weren't even inspiring. Often they appeared worn-out, negative, or sick. It was apparent to me that they'd lost their connection to Spirit. *What happened?* I wondered. *Why aren't they the way people told me they were?*

Then I had another experience: I found that I would have an excellent time with certain seers, but then when I saw them again—perhaps a few years later—I'd notice that they had slipped and were no longer in the light. In some cases, I sensed dark energy coming from them and would feel negative after being in their presence. At minimum, they were no longer people I wanted to be around, and I actually witnessed a few of them behave in inappropriate ways.

From Light to Dark

What does it look like when light becomes dark? Well, here's an example. When I spent ten years in the Christian healing tradition, I worked with a lot of priests and ministers who, in the beginning, were humble, had some amazing powers, and were connected to the Divine. But then they'd gotten too tired or egotistical (or both), and they lost their light. They looked empty, as if they were hollow shells putting on a charade. I used to spend hours observing spiritual leaders and teachers, feeling into them to see how connected they were, and I became fairly adept at these assessments.

Later, when I was in Mystery School (the name for institutions that teach esoteric knowledge and practices), I wrote a master's thesis on my study of priests and ministers acting as healers. I traveled all over the United States and visited religious organizations and events as diverse as the Pentecostal holy rollers, who speak in tongues and literally roll around on the floor; rousing evangelical tent revivals; and the most austere Carmelite monasteries. It was a fascinating, eye-opening journey as I traversed the landscape of religious Americana and examined what it had to offer in the way of connecting followers to the light, exorcising demons, and healing the sick. I wanted to observe how effective the priests and ministers were at their jobs, as well as how they themselves were holding up spiritually. As you might suspect, I found that they ran the entire gamut, from the most jaded to the most saintly, with all variations in between.

But beyond the many cases of spiritual leaders who become tired, ineffective, or sick are far-worse scenarios of revered teachers and leaders sliding into actual darkness. The news is filled with story after story of corrupt gurus and leaders from every tradition—Christian, Hindu, Buddhist, Muslim, New Age, you name it—who have been accused and sometimes convicted of engaging in all sorts of unsavory and immoral behavior, from sexual abuse and misconduct with their devotees to money laundering, fraud, manipulation, brainwashing, violence, and even murder.

For example, Christian televangelist Jim Bakker served five years in prison for accounting fraud. Indian guru Satya Sai Baba had a checkered reputation for supposed abuses, including sex with young boys. Sogyal Rinpoche—a Tibetan Buddhist lama, best-selling author, and protégé of the Dalai Lama—has been awash in controversy for decades and is the focus of a film in which multiple women accuse him of sexual misconduct. Swami Muktananda, the founder of Siddha Yoga, has been accused of sexual molestation and physical

beatings of former devotees. And perhaps most prominent are the thousands of Catholic priests who have
been accused over the last few decades of sexual misconduct with minors. Interestingly, in most cases of sexual
abuse, it's a male seer who views his followers as being
at his disposal.

I had an experience along these lines once, when
I showed up for a meditation retreat at an ashram in
Northern California. The moment I arrived, one woman
after another took me into a side room and whispered
that the seer who ran the place was sleeping with all of
the female students. He had been telling them that this
was the way he would impart to them their next level of
spirituality. I cut my retreat short after only a few hours,
finding the energy there to be much too negative.

Addiction to Adulation

So what causes those who are one with the light to
fall from grace? After a great deal of observation, here
are my conclusions.

Many spiritual leaders authentically start out in the
light. They begin with the right intentions and motives,
wanting to help the world and accomplish beneficial
things. Almost invariably, these leaders also have special abilities that were given to them by Spirit. Perhaps
they're very clairvoyant or, like Sai Baba, can manifest
gems and sacred ash out of thin air. Or maybe they have
the gift of preaching, channeling, or healing. They may
have any number of rare powers that came from an initial deep connectedness to Source. Then, gradually, they
begin to stray into the fallibility of their humanness. I

have seen one primary way that this occurs, and it's one of the main causes for the fall from grace: wanting the love and approval of their followers.

These gifted gurus and seers slip into darkness due to the allure of adoration from their "fans." They become addicted to this adulation. Of course, this doesn't only happen to people in the spiritual world; anyone who is in the public eye is at risk of falling into this trap—those individuals on TV, in the movies, on speaking tours, or in public office. Politicians, as we so often see, are particularly susceptible, as are celebrities. The difference is that we expect our spiritual leaders to be above such an addiction. Yet they fall just the same.

Here's how it occurs: you're out there diligently doing your work for all the right reasons, when you suddenly develop a fan base and the flattery begins to pour in. People love you. They think you're wonderful, and they're constantly telling you so. When you hear the praise often enough, it can be hard not to believe it. Before you know it, you're buying into the inflated picture of yourself . . . and in no time, you've fallen into ego.

Spiritual Ego

Spiritual ego is one consequence of public adulation: leaders become conceited about their gifts. Instead of remembering that they are an instrument of God—a channel or conduit for Source—these individuals start to think that they *are* Source. From here, they begin to see themselves as above the standards that society generally requires. Since they're special, they figure, the rules and regulations don't apply to them, and they begin to make up their own rules, typically losing sight of the well-being of others.

One current example is a prominent speaker who frequently gives seminars to large audiences. Although one of his main themes is helping people discover and embrace their personal power, he's not really empowering anyone. I've watched him work and can see that, for all the amazing things he does with his audiences, it's all by suggestion. He's *hypnotizing* his followers to believe that they're bigger and more powerful than they actually are. Shortly after they get back home, they return to the self-perception of being small and inconsequential again. They are unable to reproduce any of the feats or emotions that they experienced at the seminar, and instead feel ineffectual and helpless. Yet now they are addicted to the man who took them to such incredible heights. They can't wait to sign up for the next seminar, so they can regain that feeling of power.

Another example of spiritual ego, and perhaps one of the more publicized in the personal-development industry, is that of James Arthur Ray. You may recall that he was convicted and sentenced to two years in prison for negligent homicide after three people died and more than a dozen were injured in his Spiritual Warrior sweatlodge ceremony near Sedona, Arizona.

I saw James Arthur Ray in person once when he and I were both speakers at the same conference. As I was getting ready to follow him onstage, I caught the last ten minutes of his presentation. I watched as he kept lifting the audience to a greater and greater emotional peak—taking them higher and higher—until all of a sudden he said, "And you can have all of this. All you have to do is buy my workshop." Even though the workshop cost in excess of ten thousand dollars to attend, I watched dozens of people rush to the sales tables in the back of the room to buy a ticket. I could see that Ray's audience was begging him to show them the way to the abundance and financial security he was promising.

Just as there are many roads to Rome, there are many teachers who lead their students along different pathways, presumably toward the light. I'm hopeful that James Arthur Ray uses his time in prison to reflect on the direction he was leading his followers and to rekindle his desire and ability to truly help people.

Burnout

Another aspect of addiction to public adulation is that spiritual teachers or leaders may find themselves overdoing it, burning out, and even becoming sick. It can be very hard to set reasonable limits for yourself when you're in the public eye. You may be pulled by the clamor of a large number of people calling for you to help them be more.

Some years ago, when I initially made the transition from student to teacher, I was a bit nonplussed to find that two prominent women in the self-help field, who had paved the road that I found myself on, had both become seriously ill. These women had discovered some of the secrets to living a better life and genuinely wanted to pass that knowledge on to others. So why, after 10 or 15 years of being out there on their missions, were they such a wreck?

Within a year, I happened to be sitting next to one of them in the greenroom of a national TV show, both of us waiting to be interviewed. It was impossible not to notice how sick she looked, so much so that makeup couldn't hide it. She was wiped out, with nothing left to give. I wondered what had happened to her; she had been such a talented and positive force. As it turned out, I had the chance to sit down with her and ask just that, as we ended up together again in a hotel restaurant a few days later.

When I said, "You look exhausted," she told me all about how she'd committed to doing too much—that she was beyond fatigued and couldn't go on, but that she had to keep up a relentless pace to make up for several bad business decisions that had left her struggling to pay her bills.

This woman, as well as her fellow teacher who was also ill, was killing herself with frantic, nonstop activity. They were also consumed by jealousy and fiercely competitive with others in their industry. Just like aging film stars, spiritual gurus can fall into the dangerous pattern of desperately needing more fans and fearing that younger, hotter stars are closing in and trying to steal their turf. I know, I know—this is the antithesis of what one would expect from someone in the spiritual realm, but, sadly, it's all too true.

The first time I was included in an elite gathering of leaders in the self-help world, we were brought together for a group photo. I was perched on the far edge of a couch, barely in the camera frame, when suddenly the überfamous male teacher sitting next to me gave me a discreet little shove just a second before the photo was taken, pushing me off the sofa and right out of the picture! But much worse was yet to come: the next year I made the *New York Times* bestseller list and found myself positively ignored and avoided across the board by speakers and leaders in my field. Rare was the person who felt comfortable enough in his or her own fame to befriend someone as high risk as I had evidently become.

As a side note, burnout can also be a serious hazard for light bearers, even if they don't get disconnected from the light. By doing too much, they can physically burn out and bring on a premature death. Edgar Cayce, one of the most brilliant and renowned trance mediums and psychic readers of our times, was absolutely prolific in his work, but he failed to respect his own physical limits and died early as a result. That's an important lesson we all need to learn: listen to your body, the temple of your soul, and respect its limits, as it's the only vehicle you have to carry you through this journey of life.

Eva Pierrakos was another famous spiritual teacher who spread herself too thin. She made the fatal mistake of failing to recalibrate her energy field and body to make it compatible with the higher vibration that she was capable of channeling, and she essentially burned herself up.

All of the problems I've mentioned here are occupational hazards that I'm constantly on the lookout for within myself. When I first started to study healing, I worried that having the gift would throw me severely into ego. Every day when I would meditate and pray, I would say to Spirit, ". . . but don't give me the gift of healing; I won't be able to handle it. It could send me to the dark side." After a while, though, I realized that I was defeating my purpose in life. Therefore, I began asking Spirit to protect me, give me whatever gifts I was meant to have, and do whatever it takes to keep me modest.

Let me tell you, my prayers for humility were certainly answered when I went into early menopause! As obsessed as I was with my appearance back then, it was quite humbling to give up my size-two figure. The experience helped me overcome my biggest problem—pride—as I moved into middle age. Additionally humbling is the fact that, in this line of work, I frequently fail; many times, the people I try to help don't heal.

Nothing protects you from falling from grace like humility. It keeps you in check, reminding you that you're only human, and is a key to staying in the light.

Across the board, all of these spiritual leaders who fell from grace forgot what I have been advocating to you in this book: *Do your inner work.* This is the key to continuously moving toward the light. Enlightened or not, we're all still human, no exceptions. But being so should only make us all the more aware of our personal frailties and our susceptibilities to them. Just because certain individuals have made it to the top doesn't mean that they don't have to keep going through the same regimen they always have: focusing within, looking honestly at themselves, acknowledging their mistakes, doing self-forgiveness, and then working to do better the next time. Simply put, there is no graduation from the human condition, at least not while on this plane!

One thing that's strongly impressed upon you in 12-step programs is that you never graduate. Addiction is a lifelong process, and it never goes away. Once an alcoholic, always an alcoholic. You're always a drug, food, or shopping addict who is simply not using, overeating, or shopping for the moment. It's the same for spiritual leaders and teachers. Just because they're "stars" doesn't mean that they're no longer human, that they don't still have issues and personal challenges to work through. As the frequency of the problem attests, this can be very difficult to remember when basking in the glory of public success.

When Movements and Modalities Fall

Spiritual leaders and teachers are not the only ones susceptible to falling from grace; the same can happen to followers who carry on the work of a leader or teacher after he or she has passed on. One historic example is the early Christians after Jesus's death. It was only a matter of a year or two before his immediate disciples forgot that he regarded women as equals, and they began treating females as they had been for the previous five thousand plus years: unworthy to be disciples and not included in the rituals. The same tendencies still exist today, and movements and modalities can peak and later decline. The following example illustrates what can go wrong.

Reiki

Over my decades of study with a variety of teachers, I would meet someone and think, *Wow, this individual's* [or group's] *teachings are great. This guy* [or gal] *is really going to open doors for me spiritually and help me move up.* But perhaps several months or years later, I'd realize that I had surpassed them in my skills, abilities, or consciousness. This occurs more than you might think, and you could very well rise above your instructors or their instruction at any given point. That is what's happening today with this practice.

Reiki is a hands-on healing technique that uses life-force energy to clear away blockages in a person's field. It was brought to the world nearly 100 years ago by a Japanese Buddhist named Mikao Usui, who was a brilliant man of a very high spiritual caliber. Usui knew that there had to be a better way to heal than the methods used in his day. He meditated and fasted and was given a gift by Spirit that he called Reiki. My sense is that Usui didn't uncover something new; rather, he was given a technique that had already existed, but that humankind had somehow forgotten, and excitedly shared his discovery with the world. When Usui died, Reiki began to suffer, as can happen when the founder of a healing modality passes away.

I decided at one particularly stagnant point in my journey that I needed the Reiki symbols (which involve hand positions as well as phrases and other imagery) to become a more effective healer. I spent a considerable amount of money studying this art and was fully "attuned," as Reiki calls it, and began using the symbols immediately.

Not long after, I headed out to Montana for a workshop to learn how to do hands-on healing on horses. Little did I know that the weeklong workshop was at Ted Turner's ranch and hosted by none other than his then wife, Jane Fonda. As is typical, our small group of attendees began by sitting in a circle and talking about what each of us had as background training. I proudly mentioned that I knew Reiki, only to have the workshop leader, a woman famous in horse-training circles for her innovative thinking on healing, cringe and state quite authoritatively that Reiki was "rubbish" and not to be used in her workshop. I did not take this as a good omen for the trip or my newfound skills.

The next day, the leader announced that we would work in pairs. My partner, as luck would have it, was Jane Fonda. I was secretly thrilled, picturing us becoming best friends as we bonded over the behavior problems of our horses. Jane and I decided to tackle my horse first and left the workshop area to head over to saddle up Brio, the horse I'd trailered to her ranch from California.

I had purposely brought this horse, as I'd found him impossible to handle so far, let alone ride. I was hoping that, by learning and practicing hands-on healing on him during the week, and alleviating the pain that I had presumed was the source of his erratic behavior, I could turn him around and make him rideable. Alas, this was not to be: Jane and I had several nasty experiences with Brio, just trying to bring him into the workshop area. The next thing I knew, the instructor was gently explaining to me that, at Jane's request, and for her safety, she would work with another partner who had a more manageable animal. I spent the rest of the week feeling embarrassed and trying not to get killed by Brio, who I finally concluded wasn't in pain, but had been psychologically mistreated by previous owners and was totally insane.

Once back home, I did indeed spend a number of years practicing Reiki, with limited success. Then one day, a noted seer whom I was working with remarked out of the blue that I had a lot of potential but it "was blocked by Reiki symbols." I asked him what I could do, and he suggested that he remove them. The moment he did so, I had a significant initiation into higher spiritual energies, and my healing career really took off.

At one of my events a few years ago in California, a young gal joined me onstage. She said that she was actively working as a healer and longed to step up spiritually but felt stuck. I informed her that it was her Reiki symbols that were impeding her progress. (Even though this woman hadn't volunteered that she had Reiki symbols or that she had studied this practice's techniques, I could perceive them in her energy field.) While the symbols may have served her for some time, her consciousness had risen above them, and they were now getting in her way. That's what happens—your growth and abilities can become blocked by certain beliefs or practices that you have. I asked her if she wanted me to remove them. She said yes.

When I removed the symbols from this young Frenchwoman, she had a remarkable spiritual initiation right there on the spot. As you can imagine, half the room then stood up and said, "I want that! Remove mine, too!"

If you have Reiki symbols, and your sense after reading this is that they may be hindering you, you may want to think about having them removed. If you change your mind later, simply refocusing on the symbols for a week or two will bring them back into your field.

As you can see, the spiritual world is not all purity and goodness. You have to be cautious when navigating this terrain. The best way is to use your own discernment about what is real and true, about what is in the light. I can't stress enough that you never want to give away your own power to evaluate—not to anyone, no matter what his or her gifts or level of enlightenment may seem to be.

When considering working with certain teachers or taking their advice, be sure to ask yourself, "Are they real? Are they in the light, or have they lost their connection to Source?" And even if they are connected, are they too exhausted right now to help themselves, let alone you? Have their abilities waned—either temporarily or for good? You simply can't take people for granted on the basis of their reputation, as they may have peaked and begun their fall from grace. Listen to what they say carefully: do they speak about their own mistakes, admit when they don't know the answer to a question, or acknowledge when they are too tired to effect change? Those are all signs of a teacher who is still in the light.

Being an independent thinker rather than a groupie can make all the difference in your spiritual progress. Always maintain a strong amount of skepticism and an objective frame of reference. This will help you avoid becoming part of a cult or stepping into the many potholes I've encountered along my own path. And remember, while you're busy checking your teacher's ego, you'll also need to remain vigilant about your own.

The Danger of Faking It

You don't have to be in the blinding spotlight of the public eye to fall into ego. We all have a basic need for attention and acceptance; it's a fundamental requirement we have as humans. If our parents didn't do a very good job of making us feel loved, seen, and heard, in our adulthood we may look to others to give us validation. When we're not aware of this tendency, it means that it's in our dark side, where it's bound to cause us trouble.

I see examples of this in every workshop. Invariably, one or more of my students will pretend to have more abilities than they do. This is a common problem in my workshops and teachings programs. And while I do encourage students to use their imaginations, as nearly everything I'm teaching is invisible, at the same time I don't ever want them faking something to get attention. In every class, I have to distinguish between students who are actively and creatively trying to develop their abilities and those who are attempting to get me or their fellow students to notice them by appearing special or gifted.

For example, a woman raised her hand for help at a recent event, and the moment she arrived onstage with me, she started weeping and wailing and flailing her arms about in an emotional storm. I intuitively knew that this was a bid for attention as opposed to real emotions arising to be processed. Both for the sake of sticking to the truth and her safety (serious histrionics can lead to convulsions), I gently led her back to her seat and helped her regroup out of the public eye. Please be aware that it takes years as a teacher to be able to discern whether or not a student's experience is authentic.

Have there been instances where you acted out in some way or even faked it for validation, attention, or acceptance? In the quest for more light in our lives, we have to recognize our own shortcomings. And if we are going to create healing or help others to achieve greater well-being, we have to learn not only to check our egos, but we also must learn what creates healing and what doesn't. That's what we'll be looking at next.

On my way to the Brazilian rain forest to meet a healer

Pyramids in Mexico

A tribal village in the Himalayan foothills

Approaching Tengboche Monastery, 12,000 feet, Nepal

Convincing the sherpinas to take us higher up the mountain

At Namche Bazaar—on the way to the Everest base camp, Nepal

Tengboche Monastery and Ama Dablam

Waiting to meet the head llama at Tengboche Monastery

An airplane landing at Lukla Airport, Nepal

*At 20,000 feet,
close to the summit
of Island Peak*

*Camping in the area
of Mount Everest*

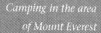

Descending through the Hindu area of Nepal

An ascetic in Kathmandu, Nepal

Buddhist prayer wheels

A Hindu temple in Kathmandu, Nepal

Ama Dablam

A holy man in Nepal

A religious ceremony in Bangkok, Thailand

CHAPTER FIVE

CREATING HEALING

"Better to light a candle than to curse the darkness."

— CHINESE PROVERB

What creates healing? What exactly do you need to do in order to heal cancer; mend broken bones; get off your medications for heart disease, diabetes, or depression; or have the energy, balance, and happiness you seek? Having dedicated my life to studying this topic, searching the world high and low for people with the answers, I can report back with confidence that *no one knows for sure!* Often, the solution involves more than just one factor and is far more complicated than we can figure out.

Please don't be disappointed by this news. I want to reassure you that everyone, without exception, has the ability to heal. The road to assisting others in this capacity is simply a very individual thing, as is illness, and what works in one situation may not work in another.

Before we delve into what creates healing, you need to grasp the distinction between what it means to help people get better on a physical level and on a soul level. Physical healing is a bodily "cure"; that is, you get well physically. Cancer goes into remission. Blood sugar normalizes without medication. Blockages in the arteries disappear. This definition is what most people think of first when it comes to making someone well, and it's the one they want to know the secrets for achieving.

That's all wonderful, but soul healing affects people to a much different degree. It addresses what's really important in life—evolving and raising consciousness, which is the true purpose of existence. We are talking about a very powerful way to heal that involves shifting from a lower vibration to a higher frequency of consciousness—moving from the lower self to the higher self, from fear to love. To use the terms that are central to this book, it's a progression from darkness to light. This type of healing will ideally restore you in both body *and* soul.

How does healing work? Basically, an energy field, or aura, surrounds and interpenetrates the human body, and this field gives rise to the physical self and serves as a living template for it. Accordingly, the body mirrors what is happening in the field. Thus, when a correction is made in the human energy field, a corresponding change will eventually manifest on the physical.

Each of our chakras (focal points of energy in the field) has its own frequency, as do our organs and emotional states. Taken together, these frequencies become the overall vibration of our bodies and energy fields. But all of us are automatically attracted to higher vibratory levels. We come from Spirit, which is an extremely high vibration, and long to return to that. In fact, when we encounter a person or place with a higher vibration, that can actually pull us up.

As a healer, I have collected a toolbox full of techniques that I have found to be effective—from ancient India's Ayurvedic system, which addresses our psychophysiology, to ancient shamanism, to energy healing. I'm a real advocate for the connection between the mind and body. In my experience of working with tens of thousands of people, I have found that what we think and feel—especially when we keep our thoughts and feelings buried or hidden from our conscious mind—affects our overall health. I have seen that certain thought patterns or beliefs tend to facilitate rejuvenation, while others are apt to create disease. When I work with individuals and get a read on their problems, I also get a sense of what treatment(s) will be the most effective in helping them get better.

What Doesn't Create Healing

To explore what creates healing, let's start with what I know for sure *doesn't*—specifically, those things that slow down the process, cause us *not* to get well, or actually create disease at the cellular level.

Negative Expectations

Here's a little story about the power of expectations and how life changing they can be. A fellow teacher of mine, Raj, has his expertise in Ayurveda. At one point, he told me this tantalizing story about his birth:

Raj's parents lived in a small village in India. Highly conscious and holy people, they led a sanctified life of meditation, prayer, and healthy eating. As a physician, or *vaidya*, Raj's father was responsible for the wellness of everyone in the community. While Raj was in the womb, his parents prayed every day for a child who could carry on the family's long tradition of Ayurvedic medicine, one that stretched back for generations. At the moment of his birth, a Hindu priest rushed in to bless him, as was the custom. He took a look at the baby and said, "He is going to be an amazing vaidya! Your prayers have been answered." Raj went on to apprentice with his father and learn Ayurveda, including special secrets known only to his family. Ultimately, he became the next vaidya of his clan.

A few years after Raj was born, his mother became pregnant with his younger brother, who was called Harshad. During the first trimester, as she took her morning walk, she would snack on mushrooms, which were in bloom and quite irresistible to her. She felt quite guilty as she ate them, though, as it is a Hindu belief that mushrooms are a low-vibration food that is not conducive to the development of the soul. When her second son was born, the priest turned pale and said, "This child is going to be dark." True to this prediction, Harshad grew up to be the cleverest and handsomest of all the children but also very naughty, and not in a cute way, as he often treated his family poorly.

When Raj was 15, his saintly father took him aside and said, "Your brother, Harshad, has caused you great sorrow and hurt you in many ways. I want to encourage you to continue to love him, but don't let him ruin your life—because he could."

When the brothers were in their 20s, after Raj had suffered additional years of Harshad's abuse, his father told him, "You should tell your brother that you will give him seven more chances, but no more." Obedient to his father's advice, Raj cut off all communication with his brother at the time of the seventh transgression and has not seen his brother for over 20 years.

This story raises the age-old question of nature versus nurture. No one is born completely dark. My sense is that it was the expectations of their parents that created the two very different paths of these brothers. Whether I'm accurate about this or not, when it comes to something as important as becoming well, it doesn't make sense to entertain anything but positive expectations.

Here's another prevalent belief or mind-set that serves as a hindrance to healing.

"It's All about Me"

We're all on a path to higher consciousness, a mission to shift from our lower-self qualities—which are related largely to our physical existence and survival—to the higher-self characteristics, stemming from the energy of love that our soul intended for us to develop in this lifetime. Therefore, it's not surprising that many of us are struggling with the major challenge of *learning to love*.

The mantra of the lower self is, "It's all about me," and we need to shift to that of the higher self—"We're all one"—so that we care about and do what is good for others. There's no higher vibration than love. Some of us understand this lesson earlier and better than others. I have found that when people refuse to grow in the direction of more love, disease is the result. Most often, it takes the form of a lack of self-love. It might show up as physical illness or, as in the next example, a deficiency in other areas of life.

One day I sat down with Suzanne, someone I've known for many years who can't figure out why her life is so barren of family, friends, and lovers, or why her health and career are a mess. Her life didn't start out that way; it eroded over time due to the choices she made. When Suzanne was in her late 20s, Spirit blessed her with a wonderful man named Doug who had two little girls from a previous marriage. His first wife had had serious problems with drug addiction, which led to their divorce and his getting custody of the kids. For my friend, who was unable to have children of her own, this should have been a dream come true.

The girls were about three and four years old when Suzanne married Doug. And although nature had put an outstanding man and two adoring children right on her doorstep—a golden opportunity to love and be loved—what did she do? She became the wicked stepmother.

Because of the hostility they experienced at home, the girls began using drugs and alcohol in their teens, trying to dull the pain they were experiencing at home . . . and this eventually led them into theft and prostitution. Poor Doug didn't know what to do. He'd always wanted them to be a family, for Suzanne to be a mother to his daughters.

Finally, when the children were both over 18, he couldn't take it anymore. He said to Suzanne, "This is no life or marriage. You never loved my children. I'm not going to stay with you." This was the exact opposite result of the one Suzanne had been aiming for all those years. She had frequently told me, "As soon as I get rid of those kids, I'll be able to have Doug all to myself." You see, she mistakenly believed that there wasn't enough love to go around; if Doug loved his children, he wouldn't have enough love left over for his wife.

When people believe that life is all about them, they refuse to give love because they want others to love them first. Actually, they *demand* it, and no matter how much is given to them, it's never enough. I remember when the children were seven and eight years old, and Suzanne assured me, "I'm not going to do anything for Doug unless he puts me before the kids." She believed that everyone in her universe was there to cater to her needs. This sense of entitlement is particularly damaging to relationships, and she's paying dearly for so many years of shortsightedness. Nowadays, she doesn't have a family to love or to receive love from in return.

My friend's disease also takes the form of financial calamity. She rarely has two cents to rub together, has trouble making her rent, and is often under the threat of having her car repossessed. Suzanne is broke and desperate, yet she still hasn't grasped what her real problem is: her selfishness and sense of entitlement. She maintains this way of thinking, no matter how clearly it isn't serving her.

Whatever our beliefs and expectations are, they're usually hidden in our dark side, in our unconscious. We keep them there because they don't reflect our ideal image of ourselves. Shame and self-blame are at the heart of this denial. Together, these thoughts and feelings are the number one obstacle I see that keep people from moving up in consciousness and the primary cause of illness. The first strategy to combat this denial and to move toward healing is becoming more self-aware.

What Does Create Healing

Thousands of years ago, the great philosophers advised us to "know thyself." And it's so true. The secrets we keep and the lies we tell ourselves create all of our disease—whether in our health, relationships, or finances. To know yourself, you must constantly be in the mind-set of self-reflection and figuring out how you *feel* about each and every thing that has occurred to you in the past and is happening to you right now. If you're continuously asking, "Why am I upset?" and looking honestly for the answer, you'll start to be in touch with your feelings moment by moment. For instance, "The reason I feel a little uncomfortable is because I was rude to that gal on the phone," "I'm feeling guilty because I'm thinking about lying to my mother," and "I'm feeling anxious because I wasn't 100 percent honest on that financial statement I submitted to the bank."

There is nothing to criticize or judge; you simply want to know and understand *you*. Then you can take the self-inquiry a step further by analyzing these sentiments: "Am I off base here?" "Is this something I need to change?" Give yourself permission to admit your mistakes and accept your frailties, because then, and only then, can you move into self-forgiveness and free yourself from shame and self-blame.

Self-Forgiveness: The Foundation of All

Healing

Self-forgiveness plays a key role in our spiritual evolution. As I've said, the number one issue blocking us from the light is blaming ourselves. Truly, it's the biggest problem I find in working with others—human beings are just too hard on themselves! I see it over and over again at of my workshops. Therefore, in addition to recognizing our feelings and giving them a voice, the most powerful action we can take to assist our healing is to acknowledge our frailties as they present themselves—to admit our humanness—and give ourselves a hearty dose of compassion. After all, a lack of self-compassion creates so much illness in people. It really does kill! And it certainly keeps people stuck in their small selves and prevents them from stepping up to a higher vibration.

How do we forgive ourselves for that abortion, screwing up our marriage, losing a job, or not being a good parent? Self-forgiveness is actually a lot easier than it may seem, and it's absolutely necessary. One of my favorite exercises to absolve ourselves from guilt is to make a quick mental list each night before going to sleep of those instances from the day where we somehow missed the mark from what we would have liked to do. Then we simply need to say, "I'm human; it's okay. I make mistakes all the time. I'm sorry, and I'd like to be forgiven, put it behind me, and start fresh tomorrow."

Next, look at what you might want to do to correct your errors. Do you want to apologize? Is there something nice you'd like to do to help your friend feel better after you've criticized her? If an apology is needed, write an e-mail, make a call, or send flowers. If amends are necessary, figure out what you can do to right the wrong. What might make the other person's life better? If you can't do something on the physical plane, do it through the ether by sending him good thoughts from a distance or perform a random act of kindness in his name. The bottom line is to be humbled by your mistakes, learn from them, and then let them go. Stop giving them power and control through guilt, shame, and self-punishment, and have compassion for yourself in this process.

Being human isn't easy. We don't arrive on this plane with an instruction manual. We learn as we go through the Earth school, and we do the best we can with what we understand at any given time. Mistakes are an important part of our evolution. I know it can be painful, but that's simply how it is. Once we're able to accept that, it will become much easier to move through the issues and wounds that are keeping us stuck.

So, forgive yourself for what you think you've done wrong. Don't stay angry or regretful or keep punishing yourself for what you did or didn't do, for what you said or didn't say. That won't serve you or the person you've hurt. Further, you won't be able to heal your relationships until you've released your self-blame; you'll continue to point the finger at others and be unable to forgive. That's because you can't authentically do for anyone else what you can't do for yourself. In this case, you'll be too busy projecting your guilt onto them!

The spiritual payoff for this kind of personal work is enormous. When you're in touch with how you feel in each moment, and when you've acknowledged all of your wrongdoings and let them go, you can rise above the pettiness of your small self. With a regular practice of connecting to Source, whatever that may mean for you—and without all of the negative self-talk—you'll suddenly find that there's space for more light to come in to your life. There's enough room in you energetically for your higher-self qualities to be downloaded from the chakras above your head and come right into your field. Maybe for you one of these qualities will be courage. For somebody else, it might be loyalty. For another, it could be resilience. The next thing you realize is that the talent you always knew you had but couldn't express begins to manifest. Suddenly, you've become a vehicle for that higher quality, whatever purpose it may serve.

This dedicated inner work is one of the primary ways we obtain our divine gifts. We become more patient and tolerant, and no longer allow outside circumstances to affect our state of mind the way they used to. Our intuition gets sharper, and we start to experience the loving qualities of our inner essence. Always keep in mind that spiritual growth leads to inner peace.

Confession

My mother knew the tremendous value of letting go of our mistakes. She used to say to me when I was a little girl, in reference to the Catholic practice of confession, "You'll thank me for instilling this in you. Something bad will happen to you someday that you'll feel is your fault, and you'll have this avenue to release the negative feelings you have about yourself." As a child, I would go with my family to confession every Saturday at four o'clock in order to be able to receive Jesus with a clear conscience and a clear heart on Sunday morning. I'd go into a confessional booth and say, "Bless me, Father, for I have sinned. I want to make my confession. I kicked the dog . . . I disobeyed my mother . . . ," or whatever I might have done. What a valuable practice to teach a child!

I learned much later as an adult that letting go of our own transgressions is an important tool for healing. It's a pity that the confession format has dropped out of practice and is hardly used in churches anymore. It's also one reason people are drawn to my workshops. I am constantly being approached by attendees who tell me the reprehensible things they have done, sensing that I can help them find a way out of that burden of shame. All of us need this kind of assistance at one time or another.

One of my favorite confession stories is from the life of 20th-century energy healer Agnes Sanford, an otherwise nondescript housewife who had remarkable abilities to create physical healing in others. During a particularly difficult time in her life, Agnes's healing abilities disappeared. When she talked about her problem to a friend who was Catholic, the person said, "You're carrying this big weight around. You need to go to confession." Agnes, a devout Presbyterian, was willing to think outside the box. She spent the next couple of weeks making a list of everything she'd ever done wrong in her life, and then took it to a confessor at a nearby Catholic church. Upon reading her entire list to the priest, and hearing his "In the name of the Father, the Son, and the Holy Spirit, I absolve you," she felt tremendous relief and danced out of the church. Interestingly, she immediately regained her healing abilities.

As a student struggling to develop my own healing abilities, I was quite inspired reading about Agnes's results and decided that I should try what she'd done. I was in my 30s by then, and I made a nice, long list of all of my sins and scheduled an appointment with a local friary, requesting that I not be given a priest with an Irish accent. I didn't tell them why, but I was afraid it would remind me of the priest who had sexually abused me as a child. I was assured that this wasn't a problem.

When I arrived, instead of the usual confessional box, I was seated at a table. Nervous, I chose to stand instead and read my lengthy list of transgressions. At the end of my confession, this priest asked why I had left the Church, and I told him that it was because I had been sexually abused by a priest when I was nine years old. He replied, "If you could forgive the man who abused you, that would be such a gift."

I immediately sensed that he too had abused children in his past and was really asking for forgiveness for himself. It turns out that even though he had turned his life around by that point, a few years later during a period in the United States when the statute of limitations was briefly lifted, this priest was arrested for his past acts with male students when he was a high school teacher. I actually felt sorry for him, because I could sense how hard he had tried to follow the Church's requirement for celibacy and how that had distorted his life. He had so much talent, and yet it was all wasted.

We *all* need an avenue for expressing our wrongdoings and forgiveness. Every religious tradition knows the value of admitting our sins, and they all have some kind of practice for it. Catholics aren't the only ones who have confession—other Christian churches have some form of it, too, as do other religions. In Judaism, public confession on Yom Kippur is a step in the process of atonement. In Islam, confession is made only to God, who is the only one able to forgive sins. In Buddhism, confessing your faults to a superior is an important practice. Among Eskimo people, a public confession is carried out by a shaman on behalf of the patient he's trying to cure, while in West Africa, the Dagara tribe conducts elemental rituals, such as a water ritual, to clear detrimental energies so that individuals may shed their issues and again be in touch with their higher purpose in life.

The Gifts of Padre Pio

One of my favorite examples of someone who utilized confession to help in healing is Padre Pio, a simple, humble Italian peasant who, from the age of five, knew he wanted to dedicate his entire life to God. However, almost insurmountable physical problems got in his way. Due to his health being so poor, he moved to the Alps where the air was clean. Ultimately, this friendly Catholic priest with a great sense of humor developed several incredible spiritual talents, which he parlayed into sainthood.

Padre Pio's greatest gift, in my opinion, was his ability to read hearts, or see into souls. He could get right to the core of people's problems at the level of their soul, below both their conscious and unconscious thoughts. He would zero right in on the one thing they were doing that was hurting them and gently tell them what it was. For example, maybe they were mean to their spouse or refused to forgive a relative. Whatever it was, he always knew. He would sometimes spend 20 hours a day listening to local townspeople as well as visitors from around the world who had come to reveal their sins to him and obtain absolution. It was one of the most valuable services he could offer those in his spiritual care. He advised everyone that confession should be done once a week, just as one would dust a room.

While reading hearts may have been Padre Pio's most powerful ability, the most famous of his gifts was the stigmata—marks, pain, and bleeding in the places on his body that corresponded to the crucifixion wounds of Jesus. When a journalist asked him if he caused these things to appear through his own mental focus, he laughed and replied, "Go out to the fields and look very closely at a bull. Concentrate on him with all your might. Do this and see if horns grow on your head!" He also was known for his gifts of prophecy, miracles, speaking in tongues, levitation, and my personal favorite, bilocation—being seen in two places at the same time. I have no doubt that this is true, and it's a skill that I'm avidly working on! I can only imagine how much more productive I'd be if I weren't spending what feels like half of my life sitting in airports and on planes.

Talking It Out

It's important for us to share our wounds, sins, and secrets with someone else, as confession used to help us do. Nowadays, we can talk to our therapist or counselor, go see the pastor at a local church, or visit with an energy healer.

It's very important to be able to express what you think you've done wrong, both in a journal you write in daily *and* to someone else. Share your guilt and grief with a friend about the affair you had five years ago that you just can't seem to put behind you. Or talk to a family member about the divorce you now regret because you realize that the person was really the love of your life and you're having trouble finding the next relationship. Whatever it is that you have done—or failed to do—talk it out with *somebody.* Declaring your failures and core wounds to another is a fundamental tool for healing. It's actually step five in the 12-step program: *Admit to God, to yourself, and to another human being the exact nature of your wrongs.* If you don't do it, as Agnes Sanford found out, you end up carrying around a lot of sludge from your past that can really keep you from moving forward, and quite possibly even make you sick.

One of the most common causes of self-recrimination I find in women is having had an abortion at some point in their past. I hear this one over and over again. They're looking for absolution, which of course I give them, letting them know they made the choice that was right and necessary at the time. You should never blame yourself for choosing not to have a child you're not equipped to raise. You have to care for yourself first; your life is sacred, too.

The other circumstance that's always so hard to forgive ourselves for is being the victim of abuse, especially sexual abuse. That's because children who are abused blame themselves. I commonly encounter adults in their 40s, 50s, and 60s—both women and men—crying because they still fault themselves for what happened when they were young. It's incredibly heartbreaking to see how someone's whole life has been affected simply because they've never been able to let go of the shame of having those boundaries breached. In these cases I make it clear, "You were not a bad child. You did nothing wrong; it was the adult's fault. You were actually a good child." This revised perspective about themselves is sorely needed for their healing.

While talking it out is incredibly helpful in resolving old wounds and releasing the regrets, self-recrimination, and other aspects of self that comprise the dark side of the psyche, there is a deeper level of healing that takes place when one is facing the ultimate challenge of life: death.

Soul Healing

As I mentioned in my book *Be Your Own Shaman,* when I was a student teacher in Mystery School, I was extremely self-conscious. I would hide at the back of the room when my teacher would be doing a healing so she couldn't call on me. Then one day, a 21-year-old girl was on the table. This young mother of two little toddlers had a brain tumor that had metastasized. My teacher, in her higher self as the ancient Egyptian goddess Isis, suddenly beckoned me up to the table, telling me to take the lead in the healing.

I started working and suddenly felt the presence of Jesus, the Master Healer, come into me and change the position of my hands in a way I'd never seen. As soon as I touched the young woman on the table, I knew that she was going to die soon, but what I was doing would facilitate her safe passage. It was poignant, beautiful, yet heartbreaking. When she got off the table, she looked radically different. She'd been on heavy doses of prednisone to keep the size of the tumor down, and the drug had swollen her face and body. Now the swelling was gone, and she once again looked like a 21-year-old. She was smiling as she said, "I'm now ready." She died ten days later, and it was a true soul healing, as was the following case.

Vincent's Soul Healing

Vincent, a fairly young man in his early 40s, had everything going for him—a lovely wife, a two-year-old son, a second child not even a month old, and an exciting career that had recently taken off in a big way. He was also a very conscious man. With years of recovery in AA under his belt, he had gained a high level of self-awareness and was mindful of what he was thinking and feeling. In essence, he was a man with everything to live for.

One day he called me and said, "I've just been diagnosed with pancreatic cancer." Of course, I knew what devastating news that was, but I was even more shocked by his next statement: "I always knew something like this was going to happen."

"Why would you think that?" I asked.

He replied, "Well, when I was 12 my father came down with esophageal cancer. He had a grueling experience that I vividly recall. It was a horrific thing for him to go through, and it was traumatizing for me as his child. He died when I was 14, and every day since then I've told myself that I was also going to die young of some terrible, dehumanizing disease—some form of cancer."

Listening to Vincent's admission, I had such compassion for him but realized that he had fallen into the trap of thinking that something that happened to his father would happen to him as well. Unfortunately, such an expectation often becomes reality, so I immediately went to see Vincent. When I laid my hands on him, I knew he was going to die, and soon. I focused my time with him on making his transition as easy and as positive of an experience as possible. Anything I did to help him on the physical level was purely palliative.

I spent the next week working with Vincent to deprogram the belief that he would suffer in the same horrible way his father had. After a great deal of effort on my part to energetically extract this thought form that was deeply embedded in his body-mind, he began embracing a new belief and picturing his remaining days as peaceful and pain free. I worked to diminish the acute fear the oncologist had instilled in him about the severe side effects of his upcoming treatment. Then one day he called me; his voice was strong and his mood upbeat. "You sound terrific," I said. "When's the chemo?"

"Oh, I had it yesterday," he replied.

"See, Vincent? It's not necessarily going to make you sick."

"Oh, the oncologist told me I'll be crawling around, unable to get out of bed—but not for the first 24 hours. This is my good day before I'm going to be deathly ill."

Hearing his words, I knew this new destructive belief had been planted in his body-mind so firmly that there was little I could do to disempower it. Despite the work I'd been doing with him to change his beliefs, conventional medical wisdom was making it nearly impossible for me to help him arrive at a place where he could heal at any level.

Despite all of this, the closer it came to the time of Vincent's death, the more connected to the light he got. I was so impressed by his expanded consciousness. He was in love with life and with everyone around him, and it was breathtakingly beautiful to behold! He reconnected with his brother, whom he hadn't seen in years. He radiated love for his wife, his son, and his newborn. He was so tuned in spiritually that it was always a pleasure to be with him.

Vincent even had a huge initiation that put in him the space of pure unconditional love. His wife was also in awe of how much he was in love with life and all those who were close to him. His friends held a fundraiser for him, and he made everyone who attended feel so incredibly loved. He didn't need anything, but he was giving as much as he could. When he died, it was without fear, in a state of peace, and surrounded by and filled with love.

Holding a New Expectation for Healing

What Vincent's doctors exemplify, unfortunately, are the kinds of problems we can create for ourselves with our mental processes. I was in my 20s and dealing with cancer when I decided that seeking a lot of medical advice was not actually beneficial because, let's face it, the news is often negative—sometimes *very* negative. If you go to doctors frequently enough, eventually you will hear that *something* is wrong, since our bodies are always in a state of flux between more solid health and moments of weakness as our systems are constantly fending off distortions, mutations, and invaders. It can be a real challenge not to latch onto a doctor's words and create mental pictures and self-talk that only worsens a situation.

We have the choice to either spend our days doing things that are strengthening and uplifting, or sit around obsessing over the latest report from our doctor showing that we've got some disease. This doesn't mean, by the way, that I'm opposed to Western medicine. Far from it. If something is wrong physically, I definitely want you under the care of a doctor, surgeon, oncologist, internist, or whomever else you've determined can best help you. What I am suggesting, though, is that focusing on negative tests and diagnoses decreases your chance of healing. When surgery, radiation, and chemo are necessary, by all means have them, but don't put all of your attention on your ailments and treatments. You want to spend your time thinking about how happy you are and, yes, even how *healthy* you are, keeping in close view all of the things in life that you're grateful for. You want to connect with the light and use your mind and emotions to co-create a new reality. You want to *use* the disease as an opportunity to release any darkness within you, to dig down deep into your own truth.

You can see by my approach to Vincent's illness that I believe it's very important to hold yourself in the light and not align with dark thoughts. What we create with our minds does have an effect on the physical world, and that's why I advise people to be careful about the information and mental pictures they allow in. Individuals who are sick need a new expectation about what is available to them, which is why I encourage them to read about and listen to the stories of those who have experienced healings. There's already way too much out there painting the opposite picture.

I remember when a doctor gave my dad a dire diagnosis. Despite my father's dark side, I had always adored him, and I was concerned about his health. It was a cold January day in Northern California, and I'd gone with him to the clinic to find out what the problem was with his neck. All of his life he'd been in excellent health, when suddenly he got a stiff neck that lasted for six weeks. When it didn't improve, I finally took him to a doctor, who ran some tests. "You have cancer, and it's not operable. It's terminal. You have six months," was the diagnosis. My father, who was always very much a believer in authority figures, died exactly on schedule, right at the six-month mark—and I mean to the day and even the minute! He was a more than willing participant in his physician's expected outcome.

Healing *is* possible, both on the soul level and in the physical body. I know that for a fact. I've experienced it myself, and I've witnessed and helped countless others do it, too. I strongly believe that people deserve this information so they can start making the changes they need to get well, beginning with relinquishing dark thoughts and beliefs and replacing them with positive, light-filled ones.

Now, here's the tricky part about disease: we can never assume that when someone is sick it means they're unconscious or dark. That's simply not the case. We all have some darkness within us—limiting thoughts, feelings, and beliefs—that we are unconscious of and that we need to ferret out and bring into the light. An illness can actually help us do that. It can show us where there's something to heal that otherwise wouldn't have caught our attention, and it can certainly be a loud wake-up call! As I've mentioned, it took a series of fairly serious problems—addictions to alcohol and Valium, a mood disorder, promiscuity, extreme dieting—before cancer finally woke me up. Disease can, in many cases, give us the hint that somewhere along the road of life we took a wrong turn. When we're sick, if we ask ourselves why, we usually know the answer. In fact, I don't think there are people in the world who, in their hearts, don't really know what caused them to become ill.

Here's an interesting story I heard many years ago. Dr. Dean Ornish, today a well-known physician, was doing his internship to get his M.D. He wanted to be a cardiologist, and as part of his studies he requested that he be allowed to go around to individuals who had just had a heart attack and ask them if they knew why. He assumed most would say, "I have no idea," but he was shocked to find that every person he asked knew precisely why he or she was ill and then gave him the reason! They would confide that it was a problem with a child, being laid off at work, or some other injury to their heart. This result wasn't at all what Ornish was expecting.

I experience this phenomenon every time I work with a group. People are constantly telling me why they're sick. Deep in their hearts, *they know*. And while everyone is different—some want to whisper it in my ear and some want to shout it from the stage—they all want to tell me because they instinctively know that unburdening their secrets will usher in their healing.

Those who have never confessed the dark secrets of their souls often find themselves impelled to do so when facing the great unknown—when getting ready to die. They feel an intense desire to unload the heavy baggage they've been carrying before embarking on that final journey of life so that they may be unencumbered and ready to meet that master teacher: death. We'll be looking at this subject more in the next chapter.

CHAPTER SIX

LIGHT AND DARK IN THE BARDOS

"Death is like taking off a tight shoe."

— EMMANUAL

We've talked a great deal in this book about the necessity of seeking light and avoiding or working through darkness. Not only is this important for the quality of our days here on Earth, but also for our experiences after death.

Why am I talking about death? Because so many of us here in the West fear that it is the ultimate darkness, the end of everything as we know it to be. The movie is over, and the screen goes black. But this is not actually what I (and billions of others on the planet) accept as truth. I believe that death is simply another transition on our path as souls, another phase in our evolution toward higher consciousness. Our lives are bookended by the major transitions of birth and death, and both involve shifting from one state of awareness to another. At birth, we come into consciousness on this plane in a physical body, the vehicle that will carry us through this lifetime. At death, we leave the body behind and go back into a nonphysical experience.

When I was a young student, I apprenticed with a seer who taught me about a proactive approach toward death. He emphasized how important it would be to remain conscious during the dying process so that I might connect every thought and emotion with the light. He said that the idea was to be meditating with one's mantra, sitting up in bed, as this would provide the optimal route for the soul's exit of the body through an upright crown chakra. This is precisely what he did at his own death; it was an incredible moment I was blessed to share with him. I felt his soul as it lifted up out of his physical self and ascended into the light. He refused pain medication to the very end so that he could remain as conscious as possible. This is my intent as well.

Death Isn't Something to Fear

As I said, most of us in this part of the world fear death. Our culture as a whole does its best to avoid even thinking about it. In addition, very few people die at home anymore. We no longer lay out our deceased relative on the dining room table for viewing; instead, the body is in a hospital or nursing home awaiting transport to a mortuary. It's like so many other unappealing aspects of life we try to avoid dealing with. For example, think of the way we tend to place the severely physically or mentally disabled behind institution walls, which is very much akin to how we put criminals behind bars. If something is wrong with us—if we're sick and dying, if our memory loss is making life difficult, if we're too old and infirm to take care of ourselves—we're shoved out of mainstream life. After all, who is going to care for us? Living in extended families is all but gone, as is the kindly widow aunt or spinster who used to look after those who couldn't take care of themselves. Everyone is too busy working or looking for work these days.

Thus, kids today grow up in much the same way that the sheltered Prince Siddhartha did—without experiencing suffering, old age, or death. It was Siddhartha's search for the truth, for reality, that led to him becoming the Buddha. Kids today may not even attend their grandparents' funerals, as it might be "too upsetting" for them. This is how we as a culture have become so afraid of death; we learn to fear what is hidden from us in darkness.

Think about how different it is for children in India, for instance. There, the cremation fires burn night and day out in the open. Young ones play around the fires and look on as the eldest son takes a thick bamboo pole and smashes open the skull of the deceased loved one so they can release the soul. They see the lepers and the lame. They still live, for the most part, in large families composed of many generations. They see what happens to those who get old and sick.

Since our culture doesn't experience death and dying as a normal part of daily life, we haven't come to grips with how to face it. Especially as we get older, or when we are diagnosed with some dreadful disease, the fear of life coming to an end creates an unnerving amount of stress.

Near-Death Experiences

I'd say that *most* people in the West are afraid of dying. The exceptions, perhaps, are those who have had a firsthand look at it through a near-death experience (NDE). Getting a glimpse of what death entails can greatly help us shed our fear.

A beautiful account of a near-death experience can be seen in the YouTube messages of Ben Breedlove, the 18-year-old heart patient who touched millions of lives when his story spread across the Internet after his death one Christmas Day. On three occasions in his young life, Ben's heart stopped and he "cheated" death. He describes those experiences for the camera, "speaking" on handwritten note cards about the incredibly bright light and overwhelming peace that bathed him in those moments. In the third event, he admits that the feeling was so wonderful that he didn't want to ever wake up. Most people who have an NDE feel this way. They may actually be disappointed to find that they've returned to their body to continue their life on Earth.

In a near-death experience of my own at age 22 (which I talk about in detail in *Be Your Own Shaman*), I almost drowned in a river on my first date with Eric, the man who would become my husband. The incredible light I saw and the absolute peace I felt—one that, as the scriptures say, truly was "beyond all understanding"—let me know that death isn't something to be afraid of. I'm expecting it to be an initiation like no other, and I've had some remarkable initiations. With this view, you can see why I'm not scared and why I don't want you adding undue stress to your life by being fearful of this inevitable life stage.

While my initial fear of death—which I think we all innately have to a certain degree—changed dramatically after my own NDE, I can assure you that there is no need to have one in order to be more relaxed about this final Earth experience. The more I spent time meditating and praying, the more I hung around ashrams and worked in the healing field, the less fear of death I had. And then one day I realized that I felt the same way about death as the seer with whom I was studying at the time—that it's just another step in our evolution. Now, that doesn't mean that I want that day to come any sooner than it must—quite the contrary, in fact. I'm simply not afraid of its arrival.

Removing the stress about dying, especially as we get older and our mortality becomes more tangible, is a real gift because it allows us to shed a concern that often distracts us from focusing on what's important and fully living our lives.

Focusing on This Life

An understanding about death isn't something you can force. It's an organic process that takes some time, and you have to grow into it naturally as you have more and greater experiences with the light. Or you can get there on the fast track, the way Vincent did by being suddenly thrown into a life-and-death struggle, where the love of life comes clearly into view and becomes the object of your unbending intent.

It's a lot like mountain climbing—you might be walking along the path at the base of the climb, not stressed in the least, just plodding along, when the next thing you know you're clinging by one finger to an overhanging mountain face with thousands of feet of air below you. As you can imagine, your whole attitude shifts instantly. That's how it can be when you're diagnosed with a life-threatening disease. Suddenly, you're fighting for your life, and it brings you to a state of awakening, because now you're really living, perhaps for the first time.

This is what I noticed about Vincent. He'd always lived a good life, but after his diagnosis he was totally present, really living every moment. Every single second was so valuable, so priceless. All he could do was keep telling the people in his life how much he loved them. It's a lot like that feeling when you're suspended out there on the overhanging cliff—in the present moment, you vividly realize how much you love life now that you're about to lose it.

Mary Baker Eddy's Take on Death

My intense focus on the present was cultivated early on in my healing career by the teachings of Mary Baker Eddy, the 19th-century healer and founder of Christian Science. I spent years studying her work, and I loved her understanding of death and reincarnation. "Death is not your friend," she often said. She believed that everything happens during your time on Earth and that you shouldn't court death because once it happens, it's final and you've lost the opportunity to utilize the experiences of this lifetime for your advancement. Of course, she was right. Your ability to evolve ceases to a great degree because you no longer have a body to operate from. You aren't able to have relationships to raise your consciousness the way you can when you're alive.

It was also Mary Baker Eddy's belief that after you die you really don't go anywhere. She felt that the next plane was a continuation of whatever you had created while here on Earth, and that this place could be either heaven, hell, or anything in between depending on how you had lived. The possibility of such a reality should be a strong motivation for all of us to work on ourselves and the issues we face instead of sticking our heads in the sand in denial of them. What a depressing thought—to die in this world only to move on and have to do it all over again, experiencing the worst of our struggles in the afterlife! Few of us would want to go through that, yet that's exactly what I find many souls doing after they have passed on . . . *if* they failed to move up in consciousness while they were alive.

Connecting to Those Who Have Passed On

Whenever souls have crossed over into the light, it's usually easy for me to connect with them, just as easily as if they were alive and standing in close proximity. I can sense, hear, and converse with them. Sometimes, though, when I try to connect with people who've passed, I find that they are in a state of limbo, as in what Mary Baker Eddy describes. Souls who are stuck in this in-between state are much harder to connect with. It feels to me as if they're in some nebulous gray place between this plane of existence and the light. In this state, they don't seem cognizant that there is such a place as the light. In fact, they often don't even seem to realize that they have passed on and, therefore, are still recycling and battling the same old issues that they weren't able to resolve or master during their lifetime.

I always equate this phenomenon with the film *Groundhog Day*, starring Bill Murray. It's a wonderful example of being trapped in an in-between state, where the same issues are continually repeated until the life lesson being dealt with is finally learned and the higher-self quality the person is trying to bring down has fully integrated. In the film, Murray's character starts out arrogant, thinking only of himself. Through the course of the movie, he relives the same day over and over again until he finally gets it right by dedicating himself to the welfare and happiness of others. As a result, he is allowed to move on to the next day. In other words, once he gets the lesson, the cycle is broken.

We can have our own Groundhog Day after death if we refuse to learn the lessons our lives are trying to teach us. To make things worse, there is no sense of time in the limbo state. What might be a moment here on Earth can feel like an eternity there. If you're dealing with your most difficult issues, this really can be agonizing! In the Hollywood version it's funny, but in reality it's something we all want to avoid. The good news is that whether we end up in some purgatory or in the light is very much within our control.

I remember once dealing with the deceased father of a client who was struggling in this limbo state. The only thing he had focused on during his time on Earth was holding on to his money. He never got the important lesson of sharing his wealth with others and was quite greedy and miserly, so when he passed on he wound up in a form of hell—where he felt that everyone was stealing from him. When I contacted him, he told me that his money had been stolen and he couldn't get his hands on it—a truly hellish scenario for him indeed.

Like any medium, when I want to reach out to a person who has died, I simply intend to do so. It's just like connecting with someone who's alive: I intend to do it. When it's someone I don't know, I contact him or her through a loved one who is still here on Earth. I first communicated with my own father in the in-between state after he had been dead for some time. It was obvious to me that he thought he was alive and still dealing with my mother, with whom he'd had somewhat of a difficult relationship. But when I encountered him again years later, it turned into a real adventure for me.

I was teaching a workshop on the East Coast of the United States, the very first one, in fact, that was being sent over the Internet via Livestream to students around the world. My revered teachers had taught me that I needed four walls and a roof to maintain the integrity of my energy field as I worked as a healer; the tradition is always to bring the energy field of your subject before you, not for you to send your energy out to them. With that in mind, I was a bit concerned about the possible outcomes of live streaming—where my energy would be carried out by my intentionality and the camera lens to points unknown. Since there were no guidelines for working via the Internet, I was in virgin territory; but being a risk taker, I decided to throw caution to the wind and go for it.

I began the event on a beautiful, warm Friday evening in Massachusetts, and I could sense my energy field extending through the live stream to students as far away as Australia, Egypt, and Japan. What I didn't count on, though I should have known, was that as I became more and more deeply expanded in a state of unconditional love, opening my heart chakra as wide as it would go, I forgot any concerns about my own safety and expanded to reach the farthest student. I merrily tripped along, not feeling any sort of problem because I never feel better than when my chakras are fully expanded and I'm working in the light.

That emotion changed dramatically, however, the minute I got home. I didn't feel well at all. I was dragging, as if an immense weight had been placed over my entire body. It was as if I were pulling a train! Clearly, something very heavy was weighing down my energy field—so heavy that I could barely walk or stand. Concerned, I phoned a colleague, a deeply connected and gifted spiritual teacher who works in the Zen Buddhist tradition (the same person who I consulted with after I worked on the woman with the cloven hooves), and asked for his help. "I have a hunch what it is," I told him. From the moment the heaviness had set in, I'd had an overwhelming sense that it had something to do with the energy of my father.

"Did you have any unusual dreams the week before the workshop?" my friend who is very intuitive, was quick to ask.

"Yes, I did," I said. "It was odd. I almost never connect with my father. He died many years ago, and I'm sure the reason I have a hard time communicating with him is that he's in the place you Buddhists call the bardo." Other traditions have their own names for it: Catholics call it purgatory or the Nether World; Judaism calls it Gehenna; and in Islam it's simply called hell, which can be either a temporary or permanent state.

For three nights before the workshop began, out of the blue, my father began to come to me when I was in the dream state. (You'll notice I say "in the dream state" rather than "in my dreams" because I don't have regular dreams anymore; I have *lucid* dreams, which are a far more aware and awake state of conscious participation than what occurs in dreams.) Even though I often visit other planes when in the dream state, I hadn't seen my dad more than once or twice in the many years since he had passed. Even on those occasions, I could barely understand him, though it was clear to me that he was stuck in the in-between state and asking for my help to get out. Despite all I had been through with him in my childhood, I deeply loved my father, and I kept assuring him in these lucid dreams that I would assist him in moving up to the light. Yet the next night, there he'd be again, making the same plea for help.

When I shared this information with my friend, he said, "When you sent your energy out through the camera lens, with the intentionality of reaching the farthest soul needing help or instruction, you didn't limit the boundaries of your energy field to the surface of the earth. Your energy, therefore, went out to other planes. Your father sensed this opportunity ahead of time and was waiting for your energy to arrive so he could latch onto it, ride it back out, and be taken to the light."

Let me offer a little explanation here: souls that don't live in the Earth realm, who inhabit another level, may be able to sense or be on two planes at the same time.

(Some of us here on Earth have also mastered this skill of being on two or more planes at once). So my dad knew ahead of time, or ahead of what we might call human linear time, that this opportunity was heading his way. And he must have spread the word around, because not only did he jump on my energy field when it came sailing out to him, but so did all of his bardo-mates. They seized the chance to have me take them out of darkness.

"You're carrying thousands of souls on your back," my friend continued. "They latched onto you when you expanded your field in an effort to help your father. When they saw the opportunity, they all jumped aboard!"

No wonder I felt so heavy! While I may be capable of taking a few people into the light at once when I'm in the healing zone, I certainly couldn't handle that many. To remedy my problem, I visited my colleague in his healing space. Together we conducted a special Tibetan Buddhist ceremony to disconnect me from the weight of these souls and lead them, one by one (including my father), to the light. When we were done, I felt a thousand times lighter and danced my way back home!

The Bardos

Various Buddhist sects use the term *bardo* to describe any intermediate state. The literal meaning of the word is "an interval between two things." I've been using this word to refer to the state of existence between life here on Earth and finally reaching the light. My experience with souls in this state goes back a long way. Even as a small child, I could sense that many people are unable to find their way to the light when they die. Later, I had numerous firsthand encounters with souls in the bardo. For instance, I used to teach energy healing in a conference facility that was located in a retirement community. Evidently, memorial services were often held in the same conference room where I taught, as the space was always chock-full of older people who were dead and gone but thought that they were still alive here on Earth. I learned to gather them up the night before I was to teach and help them find their way to the light so that the classroom wouldn't be filled with their heavy energy.

But there is more than just the bardo where souls have gone between life on Earth and reaching the light. In the Tibetan Buddhist cosmology, for example, there are definite bardos that compose the space between death of the physical body and the next incarnation on Earth.

In these bardos, those who have lived in the light will embrace the joy of their connection to Source, while those who have wandered in darkness will be filled with fear and terror at the intense radiance of the light. This is the realm of heaven and hell. Even the most wretched souls will eventually get out of the pit of hell, just as the purest souls will eventually descend again into the cycle of death and rebirth.

While traversing these interim bardos, good thoughts bring bliss, while negative ones bring great pain and desolation. The biggest problems are the difficult emotions like guilt and fear and the inability to control the experience consciously. This is why a regular spiritual practice is so important! Any practice or prayer, like the mantra-based meditation I teach, if done repeatedly until it becomes an automatic process, continues in the after-death state and affords you the opportunity to wake up in the bardos—as in a lucid dream—and move in the direction of evolving spiritually. It is also here that the thoughts of those left behind on Earth can impact the soul's journey. Chanting, praying, reading sacred texts, and performing other rituals to help your loved ones in the afterlife, especially in the first 21 days after their death, can greatly benefit them.

We need to remind ourselves periodically that we too shall die and must prepare for one of the most important initiations of our entire life, second only to birth. We mustn't forget, not even for a second, that it's this life that prepares us for our next existence.

The final bardo sets the stage for the soul to be pulled into another body to start a new life. Being born in the physical world provides the greatest opportunities for spiritual growth and realization, and choosing a good incarnation requires discrimination and some conscious awareness.

A Note on Reincarnation

I don't usually spend much time on the concept of reincarnation because, in my experience, it's this life that matters. Nevertheless, the idea that one's soul returns in another body is a belief held by millions around the globe, specifically in the Buddhist and Hindu traditions, among others. Early Christianity also embraced reincarnation until Pope Anastasius condemned it as blasphemy in A.D. 400, and the "monstrous doctrine" of reincarnation was declared anathema at the Second Council of Constantinople in 553. These days, various surveys have found that 22 percent of American Christians believe in reincarnation, as did great Christian theologians like Origen of Alexandria.

My sense of reincarnation is that it's very real, but I don't think it's linear as these traditions imply. By "linear," I'm referring to the way we humans, in our normal consciousness, perceive reality as one event occurring after another: we get up, eat breakfast, go to work, have lunch, go back to work, have dinner, watch some TV, and then go to bed. We also perceive the bigger picture as linear: we're born, we live, we die. But for those who believe in reincarnation, the cycle repeats itself: we're born, we live, we die . . . then at some point we are born again, live, and die—over and over again until we have worked out our karma and are free to relinquish the earth plane altogether, although we may opt to stick around to help others. This view of reincarnation portrays consecutive lives, but, my sense is that sometimes they may actually be concurrent, or happening at the same time.

I've had numerous experiences while working with people—during which I'm in a slightly altered state—of being on two planes at once. I'll sense two lives in the person I'm talking to, both their current one and one from the past or the future. But my very strong sense at those times is that the other life is happening right now, not before or after this one is over. It feels to me as if we have multiple lifetimes and that they are concurrent, but we just can't perceive them in that way in our normal reality.

What's the value in thinking about reincarnation? It might inspire you to realize that making a change now, shifting your thoughts or taking action in *this* lifetime, could reverberate through all of your lifetimes, not just the ones that are seemingly to come. In other words, it's possible to alter the past as well as influence the future here in the present moment.

We need to be seeking higher consciousness, making it our foremost focus and goal. This evolution is the very purpose of being on the Earth plane and is one of the main reasons I don't spend much time on the subject of reincarnation and past lives. While it can be entertaining and even fun, I see the pursuit of knowledge about our past lives as a distraction from what we really need to put our attention on—*this* life, our *present* concerns, and our relationships *here and now*. After all, even if reincarnation is a fact, the consciousness of this lifetime is the only place we can bring about change.

In fact, I find it extremely rare that a past-life issue is relevant in aiding someone today. Out of the thousands of people I work with each month, I see only a handful of individuals whose issues arise from a past life—where the key point for healing resides in the level of their field that contains their past-life material. Even in these few cases, there may be other routes that could get me there. But when no other information about the issue offers itself quickly, I will go to the level of the field where this information is stored and look for the point of entry that will clear it.

Helping Others Out of the Bardo

I've shared the Tibetan Buddhist concept of the bardo because it's a great metaphor for understanding the importance of doing your inner work while on the physical plane. That means getting to the bottom of your basest negative emotions and thought patterns—your jealousy, fear, anger, resentment, self-pity, entitlement, selfishness, and narcissism. Rather than deny your dark side, you need to accept it—forgiving and loving yourself despite your frailties. You need to know and accept who you really are, imperfections and all, and then start working to change. Denying, deflecting, blaming others, or projecting your problems onto others will lead you farther into darkness rather than toward the light.

One way to help yourself get to the light is to assist others in getting out of the bardo. This is something that religions used to aid us with back before life became so secular. In Catholicism, there was All Souls' Day, where people prayed on behalf of their loved ones to rescue them from purgatory and get them into heaven—out of darkness and into the light. Funerals back then had rituals to help the souls of the recently deceased move on. More than an opportunity to pay respects, say good-bye, or receive closure for those left behind, funerals used to be for helping the departed successfully navigate their transition. Unfortunately, most modern memorials don't have these ceremonies anymore.

Some cultures still understand the value of these practices, such as on the Indonesian islands of Bali and Sulawesi, where death is commemorated with festive funeral rituals celebrating the soul's deliverance from its cumbersome earthly shell. The funeral rites are carefully executed, since the handling of the deceased is believed to determine the soul's future course. In Mexico, the national holiday of the Day of the Dead is an occasion to communicate and connect with departed souls. Friends and family members gather at the homes and gravesides of their deceased loved ones to honor and memorialize them. They build private altars to the dead, bring gifts and favorite foods of the deceased, and share stories about the people from when they were living.

Not by chance, the Day of the Dead coincides with All Saints' Day on November 1 and All Souls' Day on November 2 in the Catholic tradition. This holiday is found throughout the world in different forms—in Brazil and parts of Europe, as well as in many Asian and African cultures. We in the U.S. seem to be the ones who have fallen behind and become disconnected from our ancestors, failing to help them make their transition to the light or to seek their wise guidance in our own lives. What do we have instead? Halloween. Talk about becoming secularized! Still, this national U.S. holiday reflects a deeper cultural connection, although mostly unconscious, to the dark and the dead. It has become our expression of that part of our group consciousness.

Another form of darkness that is almost as encompassing as death is that which can engulf the mind. The next chapter deals with the proliferation of mood disorders in our society and how we can face the darkness that sometimes pervades our minds and hearts by learning to live in the light.

CHAPTER SEVEN

DARKNESS OF THE MIND AND LIVING IN THE LIGHT

"There are two ways of spreading light;
to be the candle or the mirror that reflects it."

— EDITH WHARTON

It is often necessary to face your inner darkness and do something to increase the light inside you, to take responsibility for your own well-being, both physically and mentally. We all know people who blame others for everything in their lives. For example, my client Betsy blames everybody around her for all her problems. She complains about not being able to lose weight—and that it's her husband's fault for working long hours and not paying enough attention to her. She's sorry she didn't pursue a career and all of its rewards, which she blames her kids for—it's because of them that she didn't have time for a job. She claims she can't cope without plenty of wine, antidepressants, and sleeping pills—but she puts that on her in-laws, who are such a pain in the neck. And on and on it goes, for every single difficulty in her life.

In our culture, we aren't taught positive ways to handle our emotions; instead, we tend to use the coping mechanisms we learned growing up. If Mom self-medicated with alcohol to deal with being a single mother and making ends meet, we may reach for the wine to calm our own anxiety. If Dad exploded in anger when he was having a bad day, we may also tend to lash out over the little frustrations of life.

When Betsy's husband started to stray, she turned to a glass or more of wine every night to try to quell her fear and anger. When that didn't help, it never occurred to her to work off her anger with exercise, talk it out with a therapist, or confront her husband. Instead, she started on what became a lifelong course of avoidance with prescription medication. By the time she was 40, she was taking diet pills (easier than taking responsibility for food choices), sleeping pills (easier than meditating or exercising to reduce her stress level), and antidepressants and antianxiety medication to deal with her depression and the not-too-well-repressed anger about her in-law's interference. Cymbalta, Zoloft, and Effexor for depression and anxiety, plus Ambien every night for sleep—all of these pills threw a haze over my client's emotions so she simply didn't have to feel them.

When Betsy hit 60, she developed some serious side effects from the drugs she had been taking for 20 years. She then realized that she didn't have a clue about how she really felt about anyone or anything in her life, and she found it very difficult to get off the drugs. She finally succeeded, but it took more than a year.

What's Wrong with Taking Mind-Altering Prescription Drugs?

Since the late 80s, when the new drugs on the block hit the market—SSRIs (selective serotonin reuptake inhibitors) to boost serotonin and put you in a better mood—the medical community started prescribing them without any input from psychiatrists. Today, almost 75 percent of antidepressants are prescribed by primary-care doctors who have little training in mental health. So the basic solution to psychological problems has been to throw pills at the patient and juggle the various prescription medications until some sort of balance is achieved, usually at the expense of living with some not-too-pleasant side effects ranging from not being able to feel the highs and lows of life to lack of sexual desire, nausea, insomnia, addiction, heart and lung defects, and even suicide. Yet this easy fix goes on. As one San Francisco neuropsychiatrist put it, "Physicians have become so comfortable with using these medications, they're prescribing them to treat conditions that would have previously merited a stiff upper lip."

Today, more and more notable psychiatrists are skeptical about the benefits of antidepressants, as well as the basic idea of prescribing mind-altering meds to treat a condition that might be a social phenomenon rather than a chemical imbalance in the brain. Others feel that the vast overdependence on drugs detracts from people's ability to address the root cause of their depression, and that psychological interventions such as talk therapy are more effective than pills.

While I always recommend that those who come to see me continue to take their medications, I am very much in favor of treating those psychological rough patches with a natural approach first if possible. Before you immediately head to the pharmacy with your prescription for antidepressants or antianxiety meds in hand, pause and consider the benefits of working through your emotions, no matter how difficult. Denial and avoidance of your real feelings, which need to be acknowledged and acted upon appropriately, may well lead to a drug habit that simply numbs you. While you may not experience the lows of anxiety or anger or grief while you are medicated, you also won't feel the passion or zest or joy of life either when the low period passes. Plus, facing your real feelings gives you the chance for greater self-awareness and leads to personal power.

My Inner Darkness

I know that facing my own darkness was what put me on the path to becoming a healer. We all move along through life thinking that our minds are somehow separate from our bodies, yet when I was in my early 20s, I learned the hard way that this just wasn't true. I then went into a very frightening inner space where everything I knew became unrecognizable.

I didn't know you had to look after the body in order to care for the mind. I wasn't raised to be very health conscious. Both of my parents smoked, they weren't athletic, and there was no value placed on health in general while I was growing up, so I didn't understand what I was doing to myself during my very stressful first years of law school.

When I started, there were only five women in the entire class, and I was terrified. I had been a lackadaisical college student, and the guidance counselor had laughed when I announced in my junior year that I wanted to go into law; he told me that my grades were too low and I should consider being a secretary instead! It was only by scoring high on the Law School Admission Tests (LSAT) that I managed to get in. Once admitted, I was under considerable pressure to prove myself, and adding to the load on my body and mind I was a heavy smoker, constant dieter, and long-distance runner living on grapes, coffee, and diet soda.

At the end of my second year during finals week, a family friend in his late 40s with whom I'd been very close died suddenly. He had emergency surgery for lung cancer and never woke up. Knowing his death was caused by smoking, I decided to quit—right then and there. My motto had always been *I can make myself do anything.* So there I was, pushed to the brink by exams, dieting, running ten miles a day, and now grieving with no closure *and* quitting smoking.

Then came the final straw. I decided to go play tennis in 104-degree weather to try to stave off the cigarette cravings on my second day of withdrawal. No one else was crazy enough to be at the courts, so I spent my time hitting a ball against the backboard. When I got home, I realized I felt very odd—as if my head were full of cotton—and I fell into the swimming pool, not realizing I had heatstroke. I finally limped from the pool to the bedroom, hoping that sleep would fix everything.

I awoke at noon the next day, feeling empty and sad. My former interests suddenly had no meaning, and the next days and weeks became a blur: all I could do was sleep for 10 to 15 hours straight. I could barely focus, so I called in sick to my summer job every day, and spent a lot of time crying. My mother took me to an internist who told me I was a hypochondriac and sent me home. When I went back to law school at the end of the summer, my classmates hardly recognized me. I had gained 40 pounds and become strangely quiet. I was very slow moving, hardly functioning. I limped through the fall and winter, barely able to stay in school.

However, when the natural light increased in early spring, I suddenly recovered. I promptly lost the 40 pounds and started to become my old, hard-charging self once again. Except that within a matter of a few weeks, I was even more so. I loved it! I felt great, energized, and on fire! I started smoking again, increased my running times and speeds, and felt as if I could fly! I graduated law school and went to work at the Attorney General's high-powered office in California's state capitol, Sacramento. I was able to put in 20-hour workdays, and the guys at the office loved having me on the team. A bunch of lawyers ran every day on their lunch break, and I joined them. One insanely hot July afternoon, I showed up for the run but was the only one crazy enough to be there. With no concern for the weather, I blithely put on my running shoes and took off through the park as usual. Two miles into it, I suddenly crashed from the heat, fell to the grass, and had to be helped back home.

Again, I had the same experience as the previous summer. That night I slept 15 hours, whereas in the previous months I had needed only between four and five hours of rest . . . and I continued to need that much sleep for the next few weeks. This time, I saw the pattern of the highs crashing to the lows, as did the psychiatrist I consulted, who diagnosed me as bipolar. I was horrified at the thought of returning to that depressed, overweight, slow-moving self who did nothing but eat, sleep, and cry. The psychiatrist put me on lithium to ward off future manic episodes but, unfortunately, couldn't do anything for the depression I was currently in.

In the space of a week, I went from being a well-paid attorney living in an upscale apartment with a frenetic social life to being out of work and living in a sad basement apartment down by the railroad tracks. No one came to see me. I was already dating Eric at the time, who turned out to be a huge help for getting me back to normal. Horrified by the basement apartment, he immediately rented a cute house, picket fence and all, and moved me there. Being an outdoorsman, he said, "The outdoors will heal you," and I found that his prescription worked: as long as I stayed outside all day in the mountains with him, working for his mountain-climbing program and teaching students to hike, climb, and camp, I felt normal. But the moment I went inside for a few hours, I would promptly begin to feel depressed again.

I suspected that if nature made me feel happy, energetic, and normal, then so might other healthy lifestyle choices. I gave up my nonstop dieting and went on a regimen of eating well, making sure I got lots of protein. Instinctively, I had figured it out: poor health habits— no regular sleep, no healthy food, too many toxic substances, too much stress, and, in my particular case, too much heat—were bad not just for my body but also for my mind. Who knew the two were related?!

I eliminated all caffeine, all processed foods, and alcohol, but I continued to smoke for some time because I was afraid to quit, believing that it might bring on another roller coaster of emotions. I also stayed on the lithium that was prescribed by my psychiatrist for a while and never again had another mood swing.

It was at the end of the last depressive period when I found out I had cancer. Thinking back, I remember how much easier it was to deal with a cancer diagnosis compared with being bipolar. There is absolutely nothing as frightening as your psyche and emotions not being under your own control. Later I learned that bipolar disorders run heavily on both sides of my family. Many of my family members tried to cope by self-medicating with alcohol, and two of my cousins had been in treatment.

The horrors of my bipolar days had long faded from my mind until they recently returned to the forefront. I decided to offer a seminar on mental-health disorders for my advanced healing students and invited members of the local community who were suffering from these afflictions to join me for a day of healing. No sooner had I put the word out, when one of my closest friends confided in me that she had just been diagnosed with schizoaffective disorder, which is bipolar with hallucinations.

Needless to say, I was devastated by this news. I knew just how difficult a road it would be for her to recover, to dig herself out of a world of delusions and frequent mood swings. She'd inevitably have to change all of her unhealthy tendencies, as well as endure the frightening side effects of potent pharmaceuticals. I wished I'd counseled her years ago, instead of remaining silent when she spoke about her poor habits. What if instead I'd had a serious conversation with her about the dangers to the brain of things that seem benign, such as diet soda and donuts, zero time spent in nature, a steady dose of horror movies, staying up all hours of the night, and placing too much emphasis on pleasing others and being perfect at work? It could have helped prevent her from falling into the darkness of her own mind!

Seven Factors That Help Keep the Psyche in the Light

There are crucial elements in putting together a healthy psyche and a protocol for addressing mood disorders such as depression and bipolarity. The following seven components of an active lifestyle can help normalize brain function without the use of pharmaceuticals.

1. Nutrition

Your brain requires freshly prepared food without additives or preservatives—and if you're over 30, it needs it as often as six times a day. Your brain also requires protein, so be sure to get enough of it. And hit the delete button on nonfoods that can interfere with your mind's functioning: sugar, especially high-fructose corn syrup; diet sodas with all their risky chemicals; caffeine, which interferes with getting proper rest; alcohol, which can actually damage the brain; and nutrient-poor, processed flours and grains. Go organic, at least on the foods that really matter, specifically with oils and fats, since toxins tend to accumulate in fats. And be sure to go entirely gluten free if you have schizophrenia, as gluten has been linked to it.

There is a direct causal link between poor nutrition and depression, and there are some supplements that have been studied for their ability to aid both the treatment and prevention of the most common mental disorders: depression, bipolar disorder, schizophrenia, and obsessive-compulsive disorder. Those that have been the most studied for mood elevation and stabilization include omega-3 fatty acids found in fish oil, vitamin B_{12}, folic acid, and inositol. These nutrients are found naturally in many foods, but chances are that if you're dealing with mental illness, you may need them in higher concentrations. In serious cases, I suggest seeing a specialist who's very knowledgeable about using supplements in large amounts.

2. Sleep

Humans were physiologically designed to go to sleep when the sun sets and to awaken when it rises. Of course, we haven't done that since Edison invented the lightbulb, but this wasn't so long ago in the context of our existence. Our bodies still perform most optimally if we go to bed before ten in the evening and get up before eight in the morning. If we can't wake up on time without setting an alarm clock, then we're probably not getting enough sleep. In fact, of the tens of thousands of people I've worked with, about two-thirds feel sleep deprived to me.

The amount of rest we need depends on us as individuals and on the changes we go through in our lives.

Certain body types tend to need less sleep as they get older, and other types need more. I suggest that you keep a sleep diary for a while in order to track what's going on and note the quality of your slumber. Without enough rest, it's difficult to deal with life's normal stresses.

Here's a tip for better sleep: turn off all your screens an hour before bedtime, since the moving images on the TV, tablet, computer, and smart phone stimulate a part of the brain that takes a minimum of an hour to settle down. Spend that time visiting with your friends, reading, strolling, or taking a warm bath. And learn to take power naps, which can be one of the best ways to refill your sleep bank. Shutting your eyes and nodding off for 10 to 20 minutes in the daytime will give you the equivalent of an hour of deep sleep in the middle of the night.

3. Nature

Anxiety comes when we're ungrounded, when we lose our connection to Mother Earth. We spend so little time in nature and have "concreted" over much of it . . . I hear Joni Mitchell singing about how they've paved paradise and put up a parking lot. Yet it wasn't so long ago in human history that a connection to nature was vital to our existence. Our medicine came from plants, the stars were our navigation system, and we used animals to till the land so we could plant our crops. Now we take pills, rely on GPS units for directions, and our crops come from the supermarket.

I'm not saying that there's anything wrong with utilizing modern technological advances. The problem is that when you don't have the opportunity to immerse yourself in nature, you lose the feeling of belonging to something larger than your small self. Even an IMAX "flight" through the Grand Canyon can't begin to compare to standing at its rim and beholding the awe-inspiring grandeur.

For those individuals who just aren't the outdoorsy type, the encouraging news is that it takes very little exposure to nature to reap its benefits. A scientist at a small hospital in Pennsylvania wondered if the view from patients' rooms made a difference when they were recovering from surgery. He examined records from ten years' worth of gallbladder surgeries and found that patients who were in a room with a view of leafy trees were able to leave the hospital a day earlier than those who only had the view of a brick wall. Those people who had rooms with views also requested significantly less pain medication and had fewer problems overall.

4. Meditation and Consciousness Practices

One of the biggest problems of our modern-day culture, and a major reason so many people rely on alcohol and drugs (including prescription medications), is that we've let go of many of the things that in previous times had supported us. As I've mentioned in this book, we've largely dropped the practice of single or group confession, which used to aid us in unloading our shame so that we could be absolved and move on to make more loving and enlightened choices. Church or temple also used to give us an inspiring gathering place to connect with Source, higher spiritual beings, and others with a shared faith—but this type of worship has lost its power for many and thus waned in its appeal. In the past, priests were connected to Source and used to pass on that ability through ritual; but with the loss of that guidance, we, too, have lost our ability to readily connect.

Many of the things that used to serve us have disappeared in modern times, as we've become more science driven, technologically advanced, and secularized. How has this affected us? Well, the result of these losses is that people have become unsettled and anxious, restless and discontent. We're forever searching for something that will make us feel happy and whole. Sadly, many members of our society are in a constant state of agitation and unrest.

By now you know what I believe are the best practices for increasing your light and keeping your psyche healthy—meditation and prayer. You'll want to meditate for 20 minutes twice a day plus connect to the light through some form of prayer, whether it be contemplation, affirmations, music, art, or moving your body. An additional great practice is to write your thoughts and feelings in a journal as they arise each day. This is a powerful way to "know thyself."

Another key is to forgive yourself for your mistakes, remembering that you're only human and making it a point to make a more loving choice next time. With practices like these, it won't be long before you become aware of your dark side and begin releasing its toxic energy, helping you to avoid inner and outer turmoil.

5. Companionship

A real epidemic in our culture is the sense of loneliness and isolation that leads to depression. More people live on their own today than ever before; only 50 years ago, a mere 5 percent of the population lived alone, while now it's around 25 percent. We use the word *community* all the time, but in actuality we live amongst each other in an isolated way. We don't allow ourselves to get to know our neighbors, which breeds a lack of trust. With this attitude, it's impossible to feel safe, content, or whole, and this is precisely what makes a consumer society thrive. When we feel unsafe and disconnected, we look for something outside ourselves to make us feel whole or better.

When I ask myself, "What creates healing?" one answer that I know for sure is true, although I don't yet completely understand, is *connection*. While I realize that it's impractical for us to return to a tribal way of life, we would all benefit from building stronger connections. I've found that more healing takes place in a group setting as opposed to being with somebody one-on-one, which is why I prefer to work with large numbers of people. In fact, 20 years ago I discovered that I could be much more effective as a healer if I had a roomful of participants. Perhaps this has something to do with what Jesus said: "Where two or three are gathered together in my name, I am there in the midst of them." When many light bearers gather in one location, there is certainly a greater amount of light, which is the energy that heals.

Did you know that scientists are now wondering if we can be helped more by our connections with one another than through any medical or drug intervention?

As social animals, we have a great power to influence each other—either for good or for bad, wellness or disease. By advocating healthier choices, and supporting our friends and family members in making them, we can achieve a far greater level of health. Going toward the light means going toward love, and becoming more loving in our moment-by-moment interactions is how we heal ourselves and others on their journey.

6. Protecting Your Mind from Darkness

Follow Mary Baker Eddy's edict to "be the porter at the door of your thoughts." This means monitoring what you allow into your consciousness. Avoid scary images in movies and video games, because of the way human minds respond to those stimuli. Say, for instance, that you're walking down the street and some men in a car start following you slowly. Naturally, you'll feel threatened, your heart will start pounding, and you'll be poised for fight or flight. These hormonal responses of your body to an external threat are the biggest internal hazard to your health. Well, the same stress-producing hormones can be released in your body simply by looking at disturbing images. Whether you're watching terrifying villains on a movie screen or observing pictures of the latest disaster on the news, examples of horror and violence are extremely unhealthy, both mentally and physically.

7. Laughter

Laugh off the small stuff, since, truly, it's all small stuff! Laughter can reduce pain and stress and increase your body's resistance to disease, especially cardio-vascular problems. It can even burn calories! Many hospitals have installed a closed-circuit TV channel called the Chuckle Channel, because they've found that laughter really is the best medicine. A friend who was going through treatment for cancer swore by episodes of *The Big Bang Theory*. Personally, I'm a sucker for *Seinfeld* reruns, and I try to catch them often. Another friend attests that a daily dose of *Cheers* keeps her enthusiastic, uplifted, and looking forward to her day. Find out what works for you, and return to it often!

The Secret of Happiness

There's another important thing you can do to live in the light, which is to shift out of being concerned only about yourself. When you work through enough of your issues, defenses, and core wounds and take in enough light—giving yourself more knowledge, grace, and wisdom in the process—you're ready to participate more fully in the world. You'll be ready to do what it is that you originally set out to do with your life. I'm refer-ring to the agenda that you created before coming into the Earth plane—the intentionality you set forth about what you wanted to complete within this lifetime. This is your true purpose, and it's important to your happi-ness and evolution as a soul that you live up to your full potential, which always involves what you do for others.

Earlier in the book I told you about Suzanne, the woman whose existence was bereft of friendship and love because she refused to shift from the belief that life was all about her. Many people suffer from this mind-set for much of their lives. They're absorbed in their own little world, quite literally putting all of their attention on what *they* want, on what they think *they* need to be happy. All too often, however, those judgments are misguided. The things they're striving for are a far cry from what actually brings happiness.

At one point in my own life, I heard the call and began to change. That's the point where I thought, *I don't need all the money I make practicing law. I can just inch along on what I'm making from my healing practice.* I slowly started giving things up, because I felt so strongly that all of my attention going forward needed to be on what I could do for others.

Now, this was quite a shift for me. Let me tell you, before this decision my attention was always on what I could do for *me. How can I make myself more attractive? How can I make myself more successful? How can I make myself more powerful?* But all of a sudden, I turned a corner and went in another direction entirely. I became far less preoccupied with myself and let go of my petty obsessions, and wonderful things have happened since I've made that change. I'm much happier now, of course, because true happiness doesn't exist when we're focused only on ourselves.

I remember when my father told me that he'd found the secret to happiness. I was in my last year of law school and we were enjoying lunch one day, when out of the blue he said, "I've found the secret to happiness."

"What is that, Daddy?" I asked.

"Well, don't think about yourself. Just help others." That was pretty wise. Of course, it went right over my head at the time!

When you put others first, you're happy all day long. I never have to worry about being depressed or anxious or not feeling good because I'm always moving to help someone. When I was young, I was in survival mode, trying desperately to be a successful corporate attorney, and that didn't bring me any pleasure at all. In fact, I don't remember ever really being joyful back then. Focusing on other people enlivens us every day, because we're in a state of giving, of moving more and more into unconditional love, where our hearts continue to open. Ultimately, this creates a connection with others that just can't be forged in any other way.

Caring about the needs of others, by the way, doesn't negate the need to be kind to yourself. It's just as vital to eat well, get enough sleep, spend time outdoors, meditate, pray, journal, exercise, and take good care of *you* in general. Remember that by taking care of yourself, you'll be constantly filling your well so that you'll always have something to give to others.

Technological Connections

Like in no other time in history, today we all have the capacity to be global citizens, to touch the whole world. As a light bearer, this is both a wonderful opportunity and a great responsibility. How will you use this power? With whom will you connect? What will you say? No matter who you are or how inconsequential your life may have seemed to date, now more than ever you have the tools to make a difference in the lives of others—through your heart, your voice, and the technology at your fingertips. What's truly amazing about today's advancements is how far they allow us to extend our reach.

Sometimes, we feel disconnected simply because we've lost touch with family members and friends. We may have become too absorbed in our own hectic lives to recognize the importance of these relationships, but technology makes it easy to get in touch with long-lost loved ones. How many old classmates, friends, co-workers, or relatives have you found on Facebook or other social networks?

And there are countless ways today to *stay* connected. For example, you can share information with those you care about through phone calls, e-mails, text messages, or photo or video sharing via YouTube, Flickr, Photobucket, and similar sites. You can even keep up with relationships face-to-face over long distances through things like Skype and iChat. If necessary, schedule quality time with those dear to you. One of my friends stays in touch with her young grandchildren who live overseas via a weekly video chat. Communicating regularly with loved ones provides such a psychological boost, for them and for you!

One way technology makes it easy to share your light with others is to write a blog, which isn't as difficult as you may think. There are many websites, such as **wordpress.com**, that allow you to host a blog for free and are simple to use. You could contribute your wisdom in either an individual blog or as part of a site hosted by another community. You'll receive an amazing amount of feedback and support from others out there in the worldwide webisphere.

If you're feeling disconnected and alone, you can also start reading someone else's spiritually oriented blogs and post a comment relating your own experience to what he or she presented. If you Google "spiritual blogs," you'll come across dozens of examples. Many of them include meditations from different traditions, videos of spiritual discourses by teachers from every possible faith, and information about local groups you can become a part of. You may learn about community resources you didn't know existed and meet people who could become full-fledged members of your tribe of the heart. By participating in these ways, I think you'll soon find yourself feeling truly grateful for the blessings of modern technology.

Gratitude

Speaking of feeling grateful, one of easiest ways of living in the light is through gratitude. Gratitude is like manna for the soul. It nourishes us in both obvious and untold ways as it reverberates through our energy fields and out into the world. Like no other tool so easily within our reach, it can transform and transmute anything that ails us.

When you really understand this emotion's immense power, I'm certain you'll make it the cornerstone of your life.

The opposite of gratitude is ingratitude. Revenge is returning darkness with darkness, while ingratitude is returning darkness for light. For example, someone does something nice for you, but you stomp all over it. It's like the story of the ten lepers who were healed by Christ, and only one returned to give thanks. Gratitude is showing appreciation for what you have received and giving kindness in return.

Here's a little story that was in an ad for an online-content company that went viral across the Internet not long ago about the power of words. It emphasizes how much we take for granted and need to be thankful for what we already have:

> A blind man sat on the steps of a building with a tin cup by his feet. He held up a sign that said, I'M BLIND. PLEASE HELP. There were only a few coins in the cup, so a woman who was walking by stopped, took the sign, turned it around, wrote some words, and put the sign back so that everyone who walked by would see the new words.
>
> Soon the cup began to fill up, as a lot more people gave money to the man. Later that day, the same woman came back to see how things were going. The man recognized her footsteps and asked, "Were you the one who changed my sign this morning? What did you write?"
>
> The woman replied that she "wrote the same, but different." She'd changed it to read: IT'S A BEAUTIFUL DAY, BUT I CAN'T SEE IT.

We are more generous when we're in gratitude.

Being in a state of sincere appreciation is also the single most important tool for creating everything we want. Of course we're thankful for things we already have, but we can also have a practice of gratitude that's a lot like an affirmation but takes it to another level. Not only can you envision what you want in positive and present words—as though it already exists—but you can be grateful for it as though it has already been received. The difference is that you're connecting to the *emotion* that you would feel having your desired result, which creates an even more powerful pull on the unseen ability to manifest on this plane.

To truly transform your attitude to one of gratitude, you'll need to *practice* it on a regular basis until it gets to be a habit—until it becomes the place where your thoughts naturally go as you move through your day, including when you face adversity.

Each day, take just a few minutes to make a mental list of everything you're grateful for and, if possible, say your list out loud. For example, "Tonight, I am so grateful for my good health, another successful day at work, and the kind words from the man I met on the elevator. I'm grateful that I was kind back to him, that my favorite TV show is on tonight, that I learned a valuable lesson in my difficult interaction with my boss," and so on. You want to give thanks for the many things, large and small, that you're appreciative of—both the good things and those important learning experiences that enabled you to grow. When you make this a habit every day, you'll soon find yourself consistently thinking this way and quickly see your life change for the better.

Another option is to get into the practice of asking yourself three questions every night: "What have I received today? What have I given to others today? What troubles or difficulties have I caused?" This simple review gives you the opportunity to be grateful for the goodness in your life and to recognize the darkness that you need to clean up. William A. Ward wrote inspirational maxims in his day that made him one of America's most quoted writers. His take on gratitude? "God gave you a gift of 86,400 seconds today. Have you used one to say 'thank you'?"

Living in the Light

So how does one live in the light? Here are some tried-and-true tips for creating your best life:

1. *"Follow your bliss,"* as Joseph Campbell put it. Find the activities that put you back in the light, and do them as often as possible. It doesn't matter what your passion is—gardening, playing the guitar, or taking photos. It could be skiing down a mountain slope or walking through the woods. It may be dancing alone in your living room or singing in your car. Whatever makes you feel good and ignites your fire is an infallible way to stay filled with light.

2. *Don't give in to fear.* Fear pulls you away from the light and can make any situation worse. When you begin to feel this emotion, instead take a deep breath, exhale the fear, and remember love. If you can take whatever comes your way in stride, you'll be living in the light. And if you're able to go through each day living from the heart, you'll create a life flowing with bountiful love.

3. *Acknowledge your darkness.* As the wise ones say, "Know thyself." Examine yourself on a regular basis so you know the places in you that block the light. Self-awareness is the first step; give yourself permission to

avoid situations that make you want to be dark and appreciate the light you have. Remember, you aren't married to your family; if you have family members that makes you miserable, take a vacation from them.

4. *Keep a gratitude journal.* Oprah has been keeping one for more than 16 years. Every day she writes down five things she is grateful for, anything from fresh flowers to the kindness of a stranger. She says that by acknowledging the things she is grateful for, she stays receptive to the goodness in her life. She also claims that keeping a gratitude journal is the single most important thing she's ever done . . . and it sure has worked for her!

5. *Focus on service.* Find a way to make a contribution, no matter what you do for a day job. Volunteer to teach illiterate adults how to read. Spend some time working at your local food pantry. Stop by and chat with someone who's housebound through illness or infirmity. Call a friend who's going through a rough patch. It doesn't matter how many people you touch through your service, just spread your light in whatever arena you are called to serve.

6. *Find your life purpose.* When you're connected to your reason for being here, you'll feel fulfilled, knowing that your life makes a difference to others.

7. *Stay connected to Source.* Through meditation and prayer, or whatever spiritual practices that keep you connected to a power greater than yourself, stay focused on living in the light.

8. *Stay connected to your tribe.* Whether it's in person or via a phone call, e-mail, or iChat or Skype conversation, maintain open lines of communication with others who are aimed toward the light. Hindus call spiritual community *satsang,* Buddhists call it *sangha,* Christians call it brotherhood, and we call it Facebook. Whatever name we give it, this practice recognizes the importance of walking the path with like-minded seekers of the light.

9. *Use reminders.* Put a magnet on your refrigerator with a quote that does it for you, such as this one that's often attributed to Eleanor Roosevelt: "Yesterday is history, tomorrow is a mystery . . . today is a gift." Some people also like to put sticky notes with pithy reminders to stay in the light on their mirrors or computers.

10. *Use your unique gifts.* We're living our life purpose when we're fully engaged—mind, heart, body, and soul—and doing whatever we feel that we're born to do. Can you sing, play an instrument, dance, draw, or write? Do you have a knack for politics, religion, or the healing arts? Do you have spiritual or paranormal gifts? Do you excel at helping others become their best—possibly in a coaching, teaching, or mentoring capacity? Are you at your best behind the scenes, supporting another individual who's "onstage"? The world needs your uplifting contribution in the unique, magical way that only you can provide, and your soul, in turn, longs for the experience of self-expression that it delights in. Whatever your talents may be, utilize them so that you're living in the light!

᪥ EPILOGUE ᪥

"There is no fear in love,
but perfect love casts out fear."

— 1 John 4:18

Fear and love are the two most powerful human emotions, and they're both contagious. When you imagine what a wonderful world we could have if everyone operated out of love, it makes you wonder why so many people and organizations are busy promoting fear.

While it's important to be knowledgeable and active participants in the world, you don't want to focus too much on the negative, spending your day worrying about GMOs in food, chem trails in the sky, the amount of x-ray radiation you received during your dental checkup, the toxins in your water, or whether you've had too few or too many mammograms. Nor do you want to spend your time exposed to violence in movies and TV shows or news stories that focus on crime. Fear begets more fear. When you direct your attention to situations that engender this emotion, your energy field actually contracts, and you become more fearful. The result is that you act selfishly, without considering the well-being of others.

If you look at the world, you'll see how the atrocities committed by terrorists have escalated public fear.

Will that nervous young man seated near you on the plane blow it up? What about that guy entering the movie theater . . . is his bulky coat hiding weapons? This is fear—a debilitating state of mind that weakens your body and soul. Do you feel safer if you have extra locks on your doors, a firewall on your computer, and a gate around your community? Do more powerful scanning units and removing your shoes at airport security make you feel more secure? Or what about the emotions generated by economic uncertainty, Wall Street, big banks, a foreclosure mentality, depression, and grown kids having to live with their parents because they can't get a job?

How do we live in a world that seems to be spiraling out of control on the side of fear? How do we survive when it feels so dark so much of the time?

With love.

When you switch your attention away from fear and put it on filling yourself with the calm centeredness of prayer, meditation, and encouraging and caring for others—when you learn to share your gifts and abundance with those who need it—the emotions generated by negative images, selfishness, and scarcity disappear. The feelings of love and prosperity create cooperation and sharing, while shortage and apprehension produce conflict and selfishness. It all comes down to clearing away your personal darkness and learning to live in the light, with the understanding that the more people who do just that, the more compassion and love are spread around the globe.

What is your driving force—love or fear? The answer to that question is the basis of your life. Is it fear and darkness or love and light? If you're afraid of being alone, work on gathering your tribe. If your fear is bigger than your faith in the light, it will block your dreams and make you forgo your life purpose. If you're nervous about failing at something, do it anyway; that's courage. Doing what you're scared of, and continuing to do it, is a sure way to conquer fear.

If you need help, call on your spiritual guides and teachers. After all, everyone needs a hand at times. Fear is a habit that you can conquer with intention: *I can, and I will!* On the other side of everything that frightens you is freedom and the light of liberation. Fear serves a purpose when it warns you if you are in physical danger, and you should certainly heed that call. Otherwise, march right through and leave it behind you.

Don't worry so much about the darkness. Resist watching the evening news, turn off the sound on political commercials, and stop inundating your consciousness with fear-based images. Watch a lighthearted show instead of a violent one. Or turn off the TV altogether and write a blog, paint a picture, or turn on your favorite music and dance. Visit a sick friend, volunteer at an animal shelter, go to a workshop, or get off the couch and train for a charity walk. And laugh a lot, every day.

Your higher self is powerful beyond measure, and the light of who you are is worth sharing with the world. You can make a difference!

℘ ACKNOWLEDGMENTS ℘

With each new book, I'm reminded how much teamwork is required. There were so many who helped make this book happen.

Thank you to . . .

. . . Parvati Markus for her knowledge of the subject matter, laserlike editing skills, and enduring friendship.

. . . the entire team at the Deborah King Center: Liz, Denah, Marilyn, Sarah, and Tiffany for taking the pressure off so I could write.

. . . Jan Stake for her accounting skills and friendship.

. . . my editors at Hay House, Shannon Littrell and Patrick Gabrysiak, and the entire Hay House team for their support, encouragement, and friendship.

. . . Carl Studna for a great photograph. What a gift you have!

But most of all, thank you to my husband Eric who is always at my side. This book and my work would not be possible without him.

❦ ABOUT THE AUTHOR ❧

Spiritual teacher, health and wellness expert, and *New York Times* best-selling author **Deborah King** was a successful attorney in her 20s when a diagnosis of cancer sent her on a search for truth that radically changed her life. Unwilling to undergo invasive surgery, she turned to alternative medicine and had an amazing remission. Along the way, she conquered the alcohol and drug addictions she had used to bury an abusive childhood. Leaving the corporate arena for the world of energy medicine, Deborah mastered ancient and modern healing systems, ultimately developing a powerful healing technique of her own.

She has developed LifeForce Energy Healing and Coaching courses that both teach and transform. Her *New York Times* best-selling *Be Your Own Shaman* and *Truth Heals* take you behind the scenes and into the world of energy medicine.

Deborah is featured regularly in broadcast, online, and print media. She makes frequent appearances on national TV and is featured in *The Huffington Post* and *Psychology Today*. She is the host of *Live from Hollywood,* a spiritually based entertainment show. *W* magazine calls Deborah's work "electrifying."

Hay House Titles of Related Interest

All of the above are available at your local bookstore,
or may be ordered by contacting Hay House (see next page).

HAY HOUSE
Online Video Courses

Your journey to a better life starts with figuring out which path is best for you. Hay House Online Courses provide guidance in mental and physical health, personal finance, telling your unique story, and so much more!

LEARN HOW TO:

- choose your words and actions wisely so you can tap into life's magic

- clear the energy in yourself and your environments for improved clarity, peace, and joy

- forgive, visualize, and trust in order to create a life of authenticity and abundance

- manifest lifelong health by improving nutrition, reducing stress, improving sleep, and more

- create your own unique angelic communication toolkit to help you to receive clear messages for yourself and others

- use the creative power of the quantum realm to create health and well-being

To find the guide for your journey, visit www.HayHouseU.com.

HAY HOUSE
online learning

Printed in the United States
by Baker & Taylor Publisher Services